I0532418

LEADING WITH DILIGENCE

Leading with Diligence

TOM NEALLEY

Published by ricketybridge

Contents

Dedication   viii

PREFACE

ACT I

INTRODUCTION

SECTION I - REIMAGINING LEADERSHIP. WHAT ADAPTATIONS CAN WE MAKE TO CONFIDENTLY NAVIGATE OUR 21ST CENTURY CONTEXT?

ACT II

One	Church Leadership	18
Two	Leadership Functions	23
Three	Systems	29
Four	Clergy and Lay Identities	35
Five	What if? Communal Leadership	40

SECTION II - FOR SUCH A TIME AS THIS. WHY ARE THESE LEADERSHIP ADAPTATIONS NOT OPTIONAL IF WE ARE TO MOVE FORWARD?

ACT III

| Six | Liminal Space | 50 |

Seven	The Inchworm	60
Eight	Transformational City Networks	65
Nine	Communal Leadership across Generations	72

SECTION III - REDEEMING MEASUREMENT. CAN WE REFRAME DATA AND MEASURES FOR LEARNING TO SUPPORT OUR LEADERSHIP ADAPTATIONS?

ACT IV

Ten	Tools for Change	82
Eleven	The World of Data	90
Twelve	Church and measures, so far	97
Thirteen	Church Measurement Tools	103
Fourteen	The New Measures	109

SECTION IV - EMBRACING VISUALIZATION. WHAT IS REQUIRED TO MAKE SENSE OF AND COMMUNICATE WHAT WE ARE LEARNING?

ACT V

Fifteen	Making the invisible, visible	120
Sixteen	Dynamism	130
Seventeen	Network Visualization	140

SECTION V - CALLING. FOR SUCH A TIME AS THIS. WHAT DOES IT MEAN TO BE CALLED TO LEADERSHIP WITHIN THE CHURCH?

ACT VI

| Eighteen | Communitas and Collaboration | 152 |
| Nineteen | Responsibility and Response | 158 |

Twenty   Open Innovation and Invitation   164

ACT VII

Acknowledgements   175
Endnotes   177

To Pastor Tom

You started this. Thanks for igniting the imagination.

Preface

In the 1970's, Gordon and Mary Cosby, founders of the Church of the Saviour (CoS) in Washington, DC, famously shut down all the small groups. Gordon Cosby explained:

"...It took us two to three years to find out that the cell groups did not know how to make the transition to mission. We prayed until we got tired of praying, until I'm sure God got tired of hearing us. Finally, we just canceled all of our groups as of a certain date. We started with this new understanding."

This new understanding took shape as the mission group, which "is based on a person being called to the inward life and the outward journey in the same group. These are not groups to just strengthen each person in his or her individual mission, but in a corporate mission. So we've focused on this business of call, which is to say, 'This is God's call. I've got to do this.' We're totally committed to the inner life, the life of prayers and worship, of deepening our capacity to love, working with the blockages of love, journaling, and retreats. All of that goes under the heading of the inward life. And with that comes a real, worthy, challenging mission in the world."[1]

Practically, within the CoS, mission groups are formed by a person discerning, within community, then sounding a call. Jim Melson, the Executive Director of The Cornelius Corps (a mission group focused on racial reconciliation as discipleship birthed within the New Community expression of CoS) is an active advocate of the mission group structure. He is also a friend and collaborator. After listening to my musings, Jim encouraged me to sound a call. As a result, together we formed the ricketybridge mission group in 2013. To get a sense of the call, here are some excerpts from our foundational documents:

Local church leaders, clergy and lay, are finding their authority and value within the 21st Century cultural context diminishing. The 20th century mindset and practices in which they invested their lives, and the systems which have supported them are struggling to adjust. Every institutional foundation that has served the people well the last 75 years is suffering this.

The 21st Century culture is ripe for the fullness of the gospel as people are yearning for a foundation and meaning for their lives in a chaotic information-driven environment. Some local church leaders are yearning for the power of the gospel to refresh themselves and their ministries, but do not know how to move forward while still holding responsibility for, and grieving the loss of, what was. The good news is that God is continuing to reform the Church to answer the cries of the people of the Church and culture.

This is for those Local church leaders that are interested in learning how to navigate this journey, are willing to look at themselves as the place transformation must begin and are open to listening and depending on new and unlikely voices.

Each local church has all it needs to thrive in the future and the answers that they seek are within them, not external to them. Through embracing the ancient practices that our traditions have given us, normalizing the reality of the situation and our place in today's world, embracing the good the 21st Century and technology have created and opening ourselves to curiosity and experimentation, an adventurous journey of discovery is available to help define the Church for generations to come.

ricketybridge describes the reality of this journey and sets the expectation of what the journey will feel like for those who choose to participate. However, take heart in the words of the one who has built this rickety bridge, "Follow Me" and "Do not be afraid."

There are three foundational principles that make up the practices of the ricketybridge, which include:

- *Visualizing the Church in new ways using the combination of science, art and technology*
- *Transforming the people and systems of the church in fresh approaches to ancient ways*
- *Thinking about, researching, and discovering new frameworks for practical church approaches that bring together the people desirous of the change.*

This book is about this journey since 2013, what we have learned, and where we are going as a result of following this call. It is an invitation to the reader to join together if your heart is so moved, your mind so inclined. It is not meant to be a research thesis on the topics discussed. It is not designed to convince; but to convene those interested in further exploration . There will certainly be practical and theological disagreements. It would be great to hear them, not for argument, but for the sake of practice and learning. This book is designed to share a story and a possibility.

In Thomas Merton's *New Seeds of Contemplation* is written "The best thing you can do is write or say something that will serve as an occasion for someone else to realize what God wants of him."

That is the hope.

Seth Godin claims "your first book is just clearing your throat."

That is no doubt the case here.

Act I

I grew up in the 1960's and 70's. A truly different time in so many ways. My dad worked for the US Forest Service, so we always lived close to the forests he serviced in small, rural towns. My brother and I went back to one town a few years ago to bury our Mom and were transported back in time–not one chain fast food restaurant. We lived in Ridgway, PA at its population peak of 6,387. When we visited, the population was below 4,000. Reading the list of notable people from Ridgway on Wikipedia stretches the definition of notable. However, the town is still home to one of the largest chainsaw carving gatherings and puts on a heck of party one week each fall. My Dad was a volunteer fire person/EMT, so I remember that party well. One of my favorite memories is of a battle between fireman teams that used their fire hoses to batter an empty beer keg suspended on a high wire. It was like a tug of war, but opposite. A push of war with water. I can still see the keg flying over the head of the defeated team. My Dad was in the parade dressed as Smokey the Bear. It was a good life, as I remember it.

I've read other stuff happened in the US in the 1960's and 1970's, but not where I lived. Where I lived, nothing happened. Most notably, not a vibrant religion and/or faith.

I was aware of church, though. My Mom was an artist–an actor, singer and composer–and the local church was a place for her to share her gifts. We went pretty regularly because she sang regularly, and it's what people did, anyway. Everything else was closed Sunday morning. I got stars for attending

Sunday School class. I liked that. We got dressed up. I didn't like that. And I had to go to worship. We sat in the same pew, center/back, and I used the same hymnal every visit. I really can't recall anything that happened during the Sunday School or worship gatherings. I am sure there were seeds of faith planted. Quite covertly, though.

The hymnal, however, had blank pages in the back. A wide open canvas. On them, I began some research. For each of 1006 hymns the song writer and lyrics writer were listed. I made a chart, of sorts. For each person, I noted their contributions to the hymnal. You know those blocks that have 4 vertical lines with a fifth line slashed diagonally across to represent a group of five? There were many of those tally marks in the back of the hymnal. Lots of good work, there. A visual work of art. I don't remember who had the most, but a couple were pretty prolific. If anyone visits The First Presbyterian Church of Ridgway, PA check out the hymnals near the center back. I suspect it is still there, and then you'll know everything in this story is true.

This memory also gives a clue to my level of faith development—there wasn't much. Faith was not overtly practiced in my home so it wasn't important. And this was pretty much the case until I was in my 30's. Though I do remember a time during those confusing teenage years when I went to a youth group meeting at a local Congregational Church in Middlebury, VT. That was the next small rural town we lived in. More happened there than in Ridgway, as Middlebury College brought an alternative culture to a dairy farming community. The whole townies and gownies thing. I felt pretty much alone and was looking for something, I suppose. I had worked to get the latest new and cool Adidas tennis shoes, but that didn't help. So I ended up in this meeting. I felt welcomed and knew that it would be OK to come back.

I never did.

Introduction

Whom is this for?

Odds are this book is not for you. It's nothing personal. It's just math revealing reality. But please read on, you never know.

I've learned much of what I think about and what drives me does not resonate: long-term, systemic big-picture things. These concepts seem to come naturally to me. So whether it is a complicated mechanistic-type thing like a precision timepiece, where the workings can all be understood and solved but the project is overwhelming; or a complex systems thing like humans working together where there is so much ambiguity and unpredictability—I can't wait to dive in and question and explore interesting paths forward. If I had an alternative vocation it would be the old timepiece repairer in The Repair Shop from the BBC, or an eye surgeon. I am fascinated by that part of the human body because we can't recreate it. There is still so much yet to be learned and embraced. That is beauty to me.

I know I do not resonate when I see the eyes of the listener glaze over. Fortunately, I have had around me people who can help translate the big picture concepts into something approachable. One of my favorite pieces of advice is from another dear friend and partner in our venture, Jim Chandler. "Put the cookies on the bottom shelf so everyone can reach them." Jim is a Pastor from rural North Carolina and has a knack for taking what I think and saying it with different words and stories and people's eyes unglaze. That, too, is beautiful.

This all leads to where I am not helpful, really, at all: known problems. The kind where the solution to be applied is a best practice. When the situation simply calls for problem or opportunity identification and implementing what has been proven works. This is when my eyes glaze over. As percentages go, these problems, or how we insist on viewing these problems, are what most people wrestle with. There are plenty of excellent organizations, resources and people to assist with this work.

So, this 'not resonating' thing; it's taken some time to be OK with that. And now I am going to fully lean into it. I could say this book is for church leaders (and related systems) with responsibility for the health and well-being of the entire church and its mission. Given the number of churches and lay leadership teams, that's about 3,000,000 people in the United States. My experience has shown that when I am in a room doing my thing with leaders, about 10% respond somewhere on the spectrum from curiosity ("I want to learn more") to interest and excitement ("wow, let's do this together").

It's those church leaders whom this book is for—the 10%. The local church leaders who are called to work to create the future but are not finding support, or are looking for some alternative path forward. That is who we are. Mark Friedman wrote the book *Trying Hard is Not Good Enough*. It addresses our efforts to make true progress against social ills. We are intrigued by the title. We know it is true and are excited for another way. Others are put off by this title, taking it as a criticism; an unwelcome challenge. It is not for them, then, to pursue this work. No problem. Pursue the work you are called to do. In no way is it helpful for the Church or the Kingdom for its leaders to be out of step with call and gifting.

But for those of us that are excited to find a new path forward; we know we can't do it alone. We are in the innovation space and understand all that comes with it. And we need to work together. That's whom this book is for.

What is it about?

One of the other tips Jim Chandler gave was "don't bury the lead." Jim's brother was editor of a local paper and got this counsel from him, though I am pretty sure even he didn't coin the phrase.

Since the specific next steps are not revealed until Chapter 20, that feels buried. So here's the lead: There is a hopeful and practical path forward as those with church leadership responsibility to join the reforming work God is doing. This is a manifesto and subsequent invitation to a serious leadership pilgrimage that transcends background, experience, age and role. The problems are well documented, the path forward, in a holistic perspective, not so much. The journey is bounded by three assertions, each a movement in its early stages. We will explore each of these.

Section I asserts we must first re-imagine leadership by reclaiming certain leadership functions within our churches and related organizations. These functions have been dormant and are critical to foster Godly change. This call is based upon the Apostle Paul's encouragement to lead with diligence in the book of Romans. The Cosby's shutting down of the small groups to focus on the mission group is an excellent example of leading with diligence.

Section II explores why reimagining our leadership to embrace these dormant functions is required.

Section III asserts we must redeem the role of measurement as the critical practice to fight the power of the status quo. It is a unifying and aligning practice to catalyze the Church into the transformative Ephesians 4 body it was designed to be.

Section IV asserts we must then embrace the emerging language and power of data visualization to make the invisible work of the Spirit more visible. This tool in our leadership quiver enables sense-making of the movement of God by communicating in a way that transcends the limitations of words and numbers.

Section V explores why redeeming the role of measurement and embracing of visualization are necessary to ease the resistance of change. Within this section, we will be describing a journey rife with discovery and innovation. Phil McKinney, former Chief Technology Officer of Hewlett Packard and now innovator, thinker, author, speaker and host of the Killer Innovations podcast describes three types of innovation. We will be embracing Institutional innovation through the Leadership and Measurement assertions. We will explore Social Innovation through the activation of the Church in society. And we need to employ Technical innovation (the one we most associate with the concept of innovation)^2 in the data visualization assertion. We intend to knit these three innovation archetypes together as a pathway forward.

This book concludes with an invitation to join and engage this work, as you are, where you are, with emerging practices in leadership adaptations, developing supporting measures, and the visualization of reality. We all have something to contribute to this learning and need a space to do so.

Within the sections I have told my story in seven acts. It is how I have come to make these assertions and devote my vocation to developing them. It is the why behind the what and if I have any authority it rests solely on the fruit, such that it is, of this story.

What is the promise?

The pilgrimage will not be easy. It will be resisted. Our villain is the status quo, our insidious comforter and long-time friend. He was with us when we started our journey, and was our trusted guide and mentor. He rewards us when we play by the rules and even helps shape our identity, convincing us every step of the way that it is for our benefit. He assures us that we are helping, doing good work while simultaneously providing enough challenge and hard knocks to make us believe we are actually doing the right work.

The status quo has a vast tribe of those who are captured by the way it is. It is the majority rule. It is the air we breathe. This tribe never sleeps and does not give an inch on anything that threatens it. Its defenses are well documented in the written rules of order and unwritten cultural rules that guide our behavior. The system is so well entrenched we find ourselves being its advocate as it eats away at our health.

To live into our call means we need a leadership framework and tools that allows us to defend our efforts to change what needs be changed against this power.

Marcus is my son and is an air traffic controller. On a long drive he was musing about the role of the national air traffic system in his job. He has worked in three continents, each with its own unique approach to the same job. Simultaneously, he works within a larger international air traffic system that connects each of the systems. This is why we can fly anywhere in the world as safely and efficiently as we can. But he knows the job, itself, is chaotic. There is a plan for sure, but there are too many variables to think it will ever work according to plan. So what does he see as the role of national and international systems leaders in his day to day work? "They give us a fighting chance" is his summary.

That's the first promise of this book for us; a fighting chance against the status quo.

There is a second promise. It might feel more like a disappointment. This is not a "how to" book. It is a "what to" and a "why to" book. The goal is not to offer a proven fix. It is to build awareness and spark desire that leads to connection and collaboration. Are there ideas and thoughts and practices that we could assert? Yes, for sure. Way too many! And we will address these through the invitation in Chapter 20.

Summary: This book is for those of us who long to change the status quo but feel the frustration of trying to do so using the skills and tools we currently have, and without the proper support or a fresh path forward. There is a leadership pilgrimage we can take starting right now. It involves taking seriously some dormant leadership practices, redeeming measurement and embracing visualization. This book will explore what these are and why I believe they are the way forward. All the challenges inherent in pioneering work come with this journey.

Section I - Reimagining Leadership. What adaptations can we make to confidently navigate our 21st Century context?

Oh Lord, I am no longer my own, but thine.
Put me to what thou will, rank me with whom thou will.
Put me to doing, put me to suffering.
Let me be employed for thee or laid aside for thee,
exalted for thee or brought low for thee.
Let me be full, let me be empty. Let me have all things, let me have nothing.
I freely and heartily yield all things to thy pleasure and disposal.
And now, O glorious and blessed God, Father, Son and Holy Spirit, thou are mine, and I am yours. So be it. And the covenant which I have made on earth,
let it be ratified in heaven. Amen
John Wesley, 1755

> He handed out gifts of apostle, prophet, evangelist, and pastor-teacher to train Christ's followers in skilled servant work, working within Christ's body, the church, until we're all moving rhythmically and easily with each other, efficient and graceful in response to God's Son, fully mature adults, fully developed within and without, fully alive like Christ.
>
> Ephesians 4:11-13 - the Message

Overview

Church leadership has become more challenging than ever. It is not that we have done necessarily anything wrong. We have inherited systems and identities that are breaking down in our current context. It is now we have the choice to respond. There are adaptations that we can make today that are true to our nature as leaders within Christ's Church. It will be hard, and require us to both unlearn some assumptions and practices and learn some new functions and practices. We can start with embracing the Ephesians 4:11 gifts in a shared communal leadership practice, and begin our leadership pilgrimage with confidence and hope.

Act II

It is impossible to overemphasize the sacrament of marriage, and how God uses it. Laura is the daughter of faithful church parents. Her late father was an ordained pastor and her mom is the wonderfully caring church lady person. Bob served in the Korean War in the aide stations made famous by M*A*S*H. He became the director of Clinical Pastoral Education Department of Yale New-Haven Hospital. Avery has invested her life through serving others within the church, as a school teacher and a volunteer in non-profits.

For Laura and me, our after college life was spent in pursuit of our dreams; which had many elements of The American Dream. The church was not a big part of our lives, though it was a critical part of Laura's development. As our kids got older Laura knew it was important for them to experience the things she had, so Sundays found a new rhythm. For me, it was totally optional, and I found many Sunday mornings to be an excellent time to go to the office when it was quiet and get some good work done.

I was not resistant to faith, it just didn't seem relevant. As career development took us to new locations, churches in Indiana, North Carolina, and Georgia became part of our life. We moved to my company corporate HQ in PA, and a church community there became an important part of Laura's life. She became animated by the faith that had grounded her life since she was an infant. For whatever reason I started attending Sunday worship more frequently.

As a result, I ended up on a youth mission trip to West Virginia. I was asked to go because they need a male adult, and I wanted to go because I could be a van driver. I think I was created to be a Formula 1 driver. Not sure how I missed that. But it was confirmed when I spent a week at the Bob Bondurant School of High Performance Driving in Arizona as a gift for my 40th birthday. At the end of the week, the instructors paid compliment by saying "you really carried the mail." I still remember that. Ayrton Senna would have had more to worry about than Alain Prost if Ridgway, PA were not so remote. Anyway, I digress.

That week changed my life and I began the process (unknowingly and unwittingly) of reorienting my life towards what it means to be a citizen of the Kingdom of God as modeled by Jesus Christ. It is with great gratitude I remember the people of the church as they nurtured and encouraged my faith journey with all its ups and downs. I was an annoying, questioning new Christian. Not questioning the belief, but the practice.

Sunday morning Worship sermons began to slowly take on a new energy. Not in the preaching, itself, but in me. Pastor Tom preached with passion, zeal, and creativity, introducing two concepts that caught my imagination. One concept was the priesthood of all believers which gave me an identity. The second was that the local church in its fullness is the hope for the world, which provided both God's mission and the community to pursue it with.

I have come to believe there is an advantage to coming to faith later in life. For starters, there is not a lot of Church and Christian baggage that needs to be sorted through and discarded. And since we don't know what we don't know, it's easier to pursue the courageous steps following Christ calls us to take. I have a small stone on my desk that is inscribed with the scripture verses that guide my calling. The first reminds me of who I am, what I am, and how Jesus would have me respond,

John 21:15-22. Turn the stone over and I am reminded of what the local church looks like in its fullness, Ephesians 4:11-13. I can't recall exactly when I made this. It was part of a retreat experience somewhere on the journey. It was at least twelve years ago, for sure. It reminds me of the mysterious movement of Spirit, for who knew the influence that day would continue to have.

So as a newly minted Christian, and having no information or experience to the contrary I assumed the vision of the priesthood of all believers and role of the local church in redemption for all were true. I am even more fully aware of their truth today.

Chapter One

Church Leadership

We do not need another retelling of the problems and decline the American Church has been experiencing. We live them, read of them in books, newsletters, newspapers and blog posts. We see the relentless downward march of worship attendance despite our best efforts over the last 30-40 years. We are aware of what is being called 'the great resignation' as the realities of our situation force a choice. Since 2020, no one has been able to hide. As the tension has built and calls for change are becoming broader and more urgent the tone has changed. It's becoming less institutional, and more specific. For some of us, it's more personal.

Church leadership as a practice and even as a concept is under intense critique, increasingly by younger and future leaders. They primarily question church management practices and values, whose origins can be traced back to the business world. The world-view of a for-profit company emphasizes winning, and there can only be one winner. This is a stark contrast with the Kingdom world-view being yearned for. There is an unresolvable tension felt as the ultimate visions of these systems clash.

To succeed in a business career we are taught first and foremost how to manage. It is a great challenge to hold responsibility for a profit and loss segment of a company, every line item from the top of the P and L to the final profit is a lever over which we exert some control. The objective is delivering the famous "bottom line." Being below is unacceptable, but interestingly and counter-intuitively, so is too far above. There is a sweet spot just over the bottom-line profit budget where the winning takes place. This is not a criticism of the reality, but the world-view in which we are discipled and for many leaders, is just normal. "Don't tell me about the storms, just bring in the ship" is familiar top management encouragement in the business world.

Business leaders are invited to church leadership with the expectation that bringing the business practices to the church will fix any number of current issues. And the practices are valuable, incredible, creative gifts from God. It is the aim of the practices that cause damage. The aim of controlling (a highly valued practice in the business world) is in exact opposition to the aim of releasing (a highly valued practice in the Kingdom of God). Solid management alone will not do, and there is no better place to learn to lead than the local church.

Beyond the practices, even the need for leaders is being questioned. Writers remind us we are called to be followers of Christ, not leaders. They point out that Paul did not use the word leader much at all, inferring it is therefore not a valued function. As an example, Scott McKnight recently wrote in *A Church Called Tov* "My concern, borne out by experience, is that if we start calling our pastors "leaders," we run the risk of their losing contact with the pastoral calling and starting to shape the culture toward an institution or business run by a CEO."[3]

Further in the writing, however, it is acknowledged 'we need leaders in the church'.[4] And McKnight goes on to say they would ideally look more like pastors in leadership, not leaders in pastorship.

Though it is wise to critique leadership, it is risky to discount the unique impact of leadership. As McKnight writes "When leadership became a craze in the 1980's and 1990's, it irritated many in the church, but the irritated ones lost. I, too, chafed against the idea."[5] Inferring that it was the new focus on leadership that was the cause of the discontent. Which begs the questions: why did that focus come about? Was everything fine before this time? Or was there a legitimate problem that this response was trying to address? Was there a lack of God-honoring leadership in the pastoral ranks and systems that allowed this solution to become the craze? The adage "nature abhors a vacuum" seems apropos.

We know that McKnight is expressing genuine longing for something better. And he is not alone. What we will focus on is what can be done to address the reality that there are hundreds of thousands of local church leaders (ordained clergy and lay people) for whom this 'leadership craze' is reality, and who feel the tension McKnight articulated? There are scores of people whose lives have been permanently altered in Christlike ways by the practitioners of this craze and continue to desire it. The question to address is as follows: How do we redeem the leadership work that we have to believe was well intended that has resulted in both positive and negative consequences?

To start we will look at one of the places Paul does mention leaders and leadership; and that is in Romans 12:8c. Before that, he reminds us that we each, as members of the body of Christ, have different functions. He exhorts us to serve humbly with our 'different gifts, according to the grace given to each of us' to fulfill those functions. And 'if it is to lead, do it diligently.' Pretty succinct. Leadership is a function to which some have been gifted, and Paul gives us this summary insight into how it is to manifest. An advantage of not having multiple passages addressing an issue is that there is less room for divergent understanding. So let's dig into this one.

"If it is to lead, do it diligently" (Romans 12:8c)

One of the gifts ordained clergy bring are theological and Scriptural study to apply to practical questions. It is inspiring to see a discussion or decision influenced by the wise communication of God's truth and wisdom and watch it disrupt our normal thought and decision patterns. 'Trans-rationale' decisions are what Gordon Cosby, the small group reformer, celebrated within leadership. Clergy who were consulted on Romans 12:8c were thrilled to be asked for help on this scripture. And all admitted this is one scripture that they had not explored.

Three Greek Words

The Greek word for lead is *proistemi*. It means "pre-standing," and quoting from Strong's Concordance, *proistemi* refers to a pre-set (well-established) character which provides the needed model to direct others, i.e. to positively impact by example. It means going first and being the very thing we are leading people towards. Lack of *proistemi* is hypocrisy, a word with which we and many others are very familiar. Leadership is hard. There is no getting around that. As leaders we go first, as Jesus did by example for us.

It would be a Herculean exercise in itself to build an almanac of all the books that study leadership; especially if we include all the fields of human endeavor. We've read dozens if not hundreds of them. For now we will focus on just what is necessary that we bring with us from those well tended fields into our new territory. More on that in the next chapter.

We are more interested in the 'diligently' part of the scripture. A unexpected gift from the Greeks is the noun s*poude'* (Spoo-day' - say it out loud, it's fun). Quoting Strong again it is do things properly, with swiftness and to show zeal. To bring one's 'best' (full effort by making haste) obeying what the Lord reveals as His priority. It is pursuing the more important over the important, the better over the good; and doing so with earnest swiftness.

It is important to note there is another Greek word for diligence sprinkled throughout the New Testament: *ergasia*. This refers to the type of diligence that is indicative of process versus a product. A business-like endeavor to accomplish an end. This is not the word used in Romans 12.

These distinctions are important as *spoude'* requires us to do the right thing, with zeal, and *ergasia* to do whatever we do well. As we will explore next, these distinctions are a freeing concept to put into practice, not only when it comes to understanding how we got where we are, but most importantly, when it comes to guiding where we go from here.

Summary: The decline of the American Church is being laid at the doorstep of church leaders at every level. So much so that even the concept of leadership within a church is being questioned. Given there is truth in it, how do we move forward? How do we create something better when we are done with the critique? Scripture provides a pathway through *spoude'* type leadership diligence.

Chapter Two

Leadership Functions

Some *prostiemi* review

To frame this discussion, we need to clear the decks of some related discussions about leadership. These assertions are a foundation and are provided for clarity, a 'distinctionary'[6] for purposes of this book.

First, we say the primary purpose of leadership is to be a change agent. A steward of change. It is more art than science. This differs from management, which aims to efficiently and effectively oversee the status quo towards incremental improvement or demise. Management is more science than art.[7] Leadership must steward management skills, but transcend those to make a positive difference.

Second, we must acknowledge that the local church has organizational dynamics. There might be different visions of the organization; as an organism, a movement, a cooperative, a network, a family, a hierarchy, etc. But each of these visions has unique dynamics and expectations of leadership. But to declare organizational dynamics don't exist is a product of denial.

Third focuses on the concept of leadership styles. These are the ways we normally think about leadership. How we affect one another. This writing asserts that styles are to be wide, high, long and deep and applied with wisdom to the circumstance, mission and people involved. Not the other way around. It is not the people's job to have to get comfortable with our immutable style.

Given those building blocks, let's look at the functions of leadership.

Organization-Building Leadership[8] - *Spoude'* diligence

Organization-building leadership functions are those big picture responsibilities many us carry, sometimes unknowingly. These roles are critical as the people will not and cannot do these things for themselves. It is in these responsibilities that s*poude'* diligence is demanded for the stakes are high. These are the tough decisions and discernments providing the clarity that cuts. This leadership function determines the work of the Church.

One function is determining what type of organization any local church will be in order to serve its mission best. So people know where we fit. How this holds together. What's expected, normal and praiseworthy, and what's not. How we can contribute. We all have an inalienable right to participate, to grow, as that's what we were created for. But we will not be able to self organize without a framework to guide us. We will certainly do our best with great intentions, but the result will simply be a mish-mash of good groups and programs—nothing that will produce significant change.

A second function is discerning the whole picture; all of reality and naming it. John Seel asserts in his book *Network Power, the Science of Making A Difference* that in leading change "the first role is to define reality, so that we can work to reshape it". Reality exists across three timeframe perspectives. This presents those with organization-building leadership responsibilities the challenge to navigate these perspectives simultaneously: Using foresight to create the future; using insight to optimize the present; and with hindsight, selectively forget the past, bringing forward only what the future requires. We leaders must be able to thrive in this tension.

A third and well-known function of organization-building leadership is the whole vision thing. We've heard this is the magic elixir ad nausea. What is required here is not so much a clear or new vision statement, but imagination about what is possible. A re-imagination of our reality as though the Kingdom of God exists. A transcendent re-framing of the presenting problems of the day to to be viewed through a Kingdom lens. Not in eternity, but for now, today. It is part of defining the fullness of reality, so that we can see new possibilities and are inspired to co-create them.

As a result of this re-framing, organization-building leadership can define what success looks like, especially as it relates to changing the status quo. What we talk about and celebrate or downplay are the most powerful cues we can send to others about what is expected of them and what contributing to the vision means. Becoming crystal clear and consistent on this is a critical function.

Organization-building leadership's final responsibility is to ensure the work gets done by the right people in the right way and that it continually improves. It is not to tell people what to do. It is to create a culture, an environment, that cultivates the types of behavior that result in movement towards an Ephesians 4 picture. A familiar quote on leadership ends with "The great leader is he who the people say, 'We did it ourselves.'"[9]

There is such a thing as organization-building leadership functions. They exist whether we believe it or not. Whether we like it or not. Whether we are confident we know how to lead this way, or not. These are the leadership functions that have been dormant and need to be reclaimed. It is the reclaiming and reinsertion of these functions that will give the Spirit the ability to do His reforming work.

Execution Leadership - *Ergasia'* diligence

To further understand organization-building leadership functions is to contrast it with execution leadership functions. This is the *ergasia* of diligence. We are much more comfortable with the execution leadership activities, as this is what we were trained to do. We love people that are good at these things. We call people who do executional leadership well *great leaders.* And they are, in these functions.

To show how the organization-building leadership and executional leadership functions interact, let's look at vision discernment and subsequent implementation.. Those with organization-building leadership responsibilities discern and imagine a new possibility and the organization's role in pursuing it.

Then executional leadership functions take over. Executional leadership creates the vision statement for the website and worship bulletin. It is a communication project, trying to make something easy to remember, tangible. Good executional leadership and skills create a better vision statement for the same vision than poor executional leadership and abilities. It knows when and how to use it and why. Executional leaders develop more effective and inspiring tools to assist the people in contributing their part.

Executional leadership is the sermon-writing and presentation that inspires toward the vision. It is providing pastoral care in a manner that heals towards participation in the vision. It is providing reliable systems and processes to make administration a delight versus a burden. It is preparing rooms for meetings that when participants show up they know they were expected and something meaningful is about to happen. It is cultivating or creating teaching experiences that prepare the people for the work they were created to do. It is the singing, offering, prayer parts of the worship gathering that fulfill their unique expressions of Worship being done in a God-honoring way. It is the serving projects done in such a manner as to disciple the server as a priority of project leader, as well as the efficient distribution of goods and services. It the disruptive theology and doctrine that guides decision-making; moving from the theoretical to the practical. It is small group leading that inspires and equips people to reorient their lives towards Christ's desires. It is the leadership development effort that can multiply people to extend the work of the church. It is the spiritual oversight within the leadership teams, clergy and lay, that embodies the charism's of Christ. It is programming that provides age and context appropriate experiences that engage families and children; seniors and singles, however we choose to group people that allow them to find their place in the vision. It is the freeing of resources and assets that align to the work. All these activities are oriented to enable the change we desire to see.

We know we can do all of these things well. In these areas we have the answers and our value and contribution is known, understood and celebrated when done well. This is Church work. Important for sure. But not necessarily the work of the Church. As important as this executional leadership is, the over reliance on this *ergasia* diligence has gotten us to where we are today. The whole is less than the sum of the parts. For we know in our hearts something is missing. And what is missing are the organization-building leadership functions guiding this expenditure of energy. We will explore why next.

Summary - Leadership means changing the status quo, activating organizational dynamics and practicing humility in action. Our primary call as leaders is to the *spoude'* diligence, which can best be described in the diligence that builds an organization, in this case one as distinctive as the church. These are the functions that have be laying dormant and we are to reclaim. That is not to say executional leadership is not important, it is just not enough. Over reliance on the executional leadership functions is the cause of the current state.

Chapter Three

Systems

What is missing as we navigate our 21st Century realities is the overarching guidance of the organization-building leadership function done with *spoude'* diligence. There is a very good reason for this. It's a systemic issue more than a personal one. Though systemic dynamics have a lot to do with our identity and values, do they not? Let's explore this interrelationship.

Systemic Sin

Most church leaders, clergy or lay, grew up with and are trained with the following assumptions undergirding everything: It is good for people to be Christians for their own sake. Christians also make the world a better place to live. Christians are formed by going to "church." By doing the functions of church well, we will have more, better formed Christians. Therefore the world will look more and more like God desires. We assume a virtuous cycle fueled by our church activities.

These assumptions undergird our preparation for church leadership. As an example here is the list of training and ministry competence areas for the pastors and leaders of a church network formed in 2022:

Character - maturity of faith, personal integrity, understanding of and adherence to pastoral ethics, affirm the standards and care values of the network.

Skills and Knowledge - Biblical Interpretation, Understanding of Old and New Testaments, Reformed theology and church practice, theology and administration of the sacraments, church history, ability to preach and teach, capacity to lead and minister within the church.

The training in these areas could come through a formal educations (eg. Seminary) or alternative tracks, and competency in these areas will be demonstrated through examinations, papers, and experiences.

This training is representative of the power of the system of church we inherited, the status quo, the air we breathe. These attributes are not bad in themselves, they are just incomplete, which is part of the danger. Nowhere in this curriculum will the organization-building leadership functions be addressed. The competencies listed are the hallmarks of the past. The new network founders are repeating what is known and what they themselves likely embody. It is an excellent example of how the status quo continues its destructive onslaught on the Church while God is moving to reformation. How does this happen and why would they do this?

It is primarily a case of not being aware that this time in history demands new leadership skills and qualifications. We have functioned well enough without them over the past few generations. The church systems institutionalized these functions on our behalf, so we just needed to execute as directed. The organizational leadership aspects of the church were codified sometime in the distant past through books of church order, books of discipline, by-laws, etc. Even if the system was not formalized, the informal approaches mirror the intent and purpose. They are locked in stone, and well defended formally and informally, which make them highly resistant to change.

The unintended consequence is that we were not trained to be aware of or value the organization-building leadership functions, much less be proficient in them. These leadership functions were optional, or someone else's responsibility. We might even contend they were not necessary at the time. Some would still contend that today.

But we were warned of this. Mike Regele, author of *Death of the Church* in 1995 wrote, as he was looking forward to today, "There is not dearth of leaders to fill positions of leadership. The dearth is of leaders who have the kind of qualities necessary to provide the type of leadership that will be required."[10]

The times have changed, but the training and value systems have not. So here we are unequipped to employ organization-building leadership functions when the current climate demands them. We know we have to unlearn and relearn; we can say the words. But like following Jesus, it is very difficult to do.

Identity

We must also ask ourselves; do we see the organization-building leadership role as a part of our identity? Do we believe we are gifted and called to this type of work and responsibility? Or are we just the preacher? Or are we just the laity? Or if we just focus on becoming more like Jesus, do we believe it will all work out? Isn't being a servant leader good enough?

Let's tackle that last question first. We need to take a quick detour back to the *proistemi* part of lead with diligence. For servant leadership isn't so much about being diligent as it is who we are.

We are inundated with the ideal of servant leadership. And it's right to be as this is how Jesus led. It's precisely who he is. It is exactly what Paul encourages us to do repeatedly in the letters to the churches. It is the posture we could adopt in every interaction with all people. It is mandatory if the church will live anywhere into its full potential. Servant-hood is practiced in healthy and intentional discipleship processes, programs and prayer. It is an outcome of Christ's work in our lives together more than an alternative leadership style or approach. Servant leadership exists and has power because mature servants are performing leadership functions.

"Servant leadership fundamentally counter the savior-hero leader, who single handedly saves the day. Rather, the servant leader humbly empowers others to save the day, and is hardily noticed until he or she is missing. Servant Leadership empowers and transforms - it does not control and dominate"[11] Bishop Grant Hiyaga succinctly summed up in his book *Spiritual Kaizan.*

The status quo has devised an elegant trap when we emphasize servanthood as a leadership style or a training program—a 'how to' instead of a 'who to.' It's easy to get enamored in focusing on the servant part as it feels good to everyone. It's in our DNA. It's a beautiful paradox that when we serve, all involved grow in depth and connection. Synergy, we call it. Love. So, just do more of that, right? Just be a servant and hope for the best.

The trap? It's the second word in servant leadership that loses out: leadership. What and whom we are in leading in this servant posture? Where are we leading toward? Servanthood is awesome, unless it is used to avoid accountability. Organization-building leadership is a responsibility to which we are accountable. When Jesus washed the feet of his closest disciples it was an act to prepare them for the future leadership roles they had ahead of them. To show them who they were to be as they were sent to their organization-building functions. To prepare them to tackle the status quo of the day for the good of all people. It was part of intentional, daily organization-building practice which has resulted in us sharing in those responsibilities today. We could employ the best of organization-building leadership skills, but without the posture of servanthood they have no power. Alternatively, we could practice servanthood in all activities, but without employing organization-building leadership skills we disperse and weaken the power. Either the way the status quo stays intact.

Paul addressed this when he was writing to the Church in Rome. Paraphrasing some more of Romans 12. Do not think of yourself more highly than you ought (servant leadership). There are many functions in the church, and the members have been given the Gifts to perform them. If your gift is leading, do it diligently (organization-building leadership).

Servant leadership is who we are in our role, whether we are performing organization building functions, executional leadership functions or management functions. It is our character, our virtue and a result of our communal discipleship practices and desire.

Many of us have found ourselves in a position where we must take on this organization-building responsibility. As we've mentioned, it's not everyone's responsibility. It's for those given the gift of *spoude'* diligence. Or for those of us who have willingly (or unwittingly) accepted the responsibility. Many of us find ourselves with these responsibilities without ever being told they are part of the role.

"But I'm just the preacher."

"But I'm just a lay person."

These are two phrases we've heard too often in our leadership spaces. They are heartbreaking. The 'just' part. They are sometimes even said out loud for all to hear. They are often a refrain echoing in our collective heads. They are many times disguised through silence.

These phrases can come from an internal insecurity about our seat at the table, or the particular area of discussion. Or they come from an external system of caste or hierarchy that keeps people in their place. Neither phrase is consistent with our birthright as Children of God, imbued with gifts and calling, nor consistent with the body of Christ working in unity.

Organization-building leadership is a high calling ordained by God, not to be apologized for but stewarded well for the benefit of others to the Glory of God. Our gifts and skills in this area are developed, encouraged and refined through the crucible of ministry with others. Can we accept this as we are gifted and called? Are we willing to say yes to the invitation? This invitation transcends the status-quo's most powerful identity system, that of clergy and lay people of the Church. We will attend to that next.

Summary. The current state, the status quo, is protected and defended by the systems we have in place. They may be formal as in our organizational documents or informal as part of shared beliefs and assumptions, but they trap us nonetheless. A more devious trap is substituting the posture of servant leadership for the functions of leadership. It feels really right in the church setting and can become the end in itself. A third defense mechanism we of the status quo is the belittling of our identity within the leadership systems.

Chapter Four

Clergy and Lay Identities

Let's assume we can accept the calling God has entrusted with us. We must then consider that this leadership function can only be accomplished in deep collaboration with others. It is a group endeavor. And that is good news. To explore this we must dive deeper into the challenge these two identities present us.

Jesus Christ is the head of the Church. He has entrusted the leadership of the Church to those he gifted. To lead diligently. Jesus does not, nor did he ever, expect this leadership to come from one person. This is where our beliefs and practice say we disagree with Him. We prefer the individual human leader, and our systems have anointed the pastor as that leader. We've created a fragile system with a single point of failure. Church leadership was designed as a group activity.

The Clergy

Is there a vocation that is more misunderstood? "It must be nice working half a day a week." is an oft repeated jest.

"Funerals, weddings, public gatherings, invocations, worship, preaching and special programs—the list goes on and on. In fact, there are probably very few professions that call upon such a diverse and varied set of roles and duties," write Richard DeShon and Abigail Quinn, two Michigan State university researchers who study the role of clergy. DeShon and Quinn commented "that they had never seen another profession where individuals had to switch roles so often and so quickly. And [they] were surprised at the sheer number of role and duties that comes with pastoral ministry."[12]

Additionally, we expect pastors to not only be agile in performing tasks, but in displaying the gifts of Apostle, Prophet, Evangelist, Shepard and Teacher. We are asking them to be Jesus.

Despite the expectations, ordained or appointed pastors willingly say yes to this vocation. One that is famous for being paid very little. Especially given what they might earn given the educational investment required.

And it used to be worth it. It used to make sense. The role was valued. The pastor(s) of the local church were always parts of the discussions of the future of the town or city. The people who worshiped on Sundays were well read in biblical understanding and the preaching helped people grow. Sunday mornings were a protected time by culture for the worship of God. Despite the low compensation, the church assured a pastor's housing, long-term health care and pension. All these things are are now in question.

We saw it one Monday morning at a denominational meeting. Larry was the Pastor at a local church, and he had to share. He reported that for just one Sunday morning his usual routine was interrupted. He went to brunch with his family over an out-of-town wedding weekend. There were people everywhere. Enjoying themselves, loving life. He was shocked. He had somehow come to the belief that everyone was either going to worship with another church, or alternatively just lazing at home. But then the statistics, the relentless marching downward of the percentage of people attending Sunday worship attendance, finally, became excruciatingly real. They were not at any church, and not lazing at home. They had life and were happy, very happy. It hit him. "We are, irrelevant" he said. He wept. Something has died.

The Lay Leaders

Every Church has them of some sort. Though as much as pastors are asked to be too much like Jesus, our lay leadership is not asked enough to be like Jesus. I don't think this is on purpose. It's not anyone's fault. It is just an unintended consequence of our systems and focus on executional leadership. This happened out of practical necessity.

Bishop Hagiya says "as much as clergy are trained in the empathy-service side of ministry (and teaching), the opposite is probably true of the other dimension of social awareness, which is defined as "reading the currents, decision networks, and politics at the organizational level." Clearly this is not a strength or major concern of most seminary curriculum. "Clergy are ill-equipped to deal with the organizational side of church..." [13]

So we have created an artificial dualism in church leadership. The lay leaders are tasked to handle the 'temporal' side of the church. Committees or teams have full authority or are strong advisers to the Pastor. The Pastors will handle the spiritual side of things. This kind of thinking enables the aforementioned "I'm just a pastor or just lay person" identity crisis by giving complete say in these areas to those who are supposedly the experts. As a result, the Pastor is not expected to bring theological reflection and discernment capability or practice to temporal issues and the lay leaders are not expected to bring organizational perspectives and practices to the spiritual side of things. It's as if these perspectives are disconnected and not interdependent.

The issues here manifest themselves in a couple of ways. Related to organizational principles, the experiences and preferences of lay leadership can end up driving the organizational system. "Well, in the military we learned that this, this, and this is the way things work, so that's what we should be doing". Substitute for military the business world, start up community, school system, nonprofit, government, my other church, etc.

Then when important decisions need to be made, the lay leadership votes to do it a certain way and the pastor goes along, many times despite a sense of spiritual distress. *"It's what the board has decided, what can I say?"*

Alternatively, the lay leadership may be unwilling to take a stand, strong opinions notwithstanding; and go along with the pastor's decision, despite terrible reservations. *"It's what the pastor wanted, what can we say?"*

These cycles foster an astonishingly strong co-dependency. I was part of a two day off-site leadership organizational retreat focused on changes a local church needed. It was clear to all in attendance that the Senior Pastor did not have the required skills to lead into the changes necessary. He vulnerably agreed that he would have to take some important direction from lay staff and leadership. However, the Senior Pastor never had the chance to do so. The lay leaders were "uncomfortable with strategy not coming from the Senior Pastor." As a result, they decided to keep what was known to be broken instead of making the necessary changes. All were pleased. "Good meeting" was the closing chorus. The status quo rejoiced.

Systems again

We are aware there is a problem. As leaders we have therefore traditionally focused on trying to develop the pastor. Most every podcast, blog, conference and book on leadership development focuses on changing the pastor, and is written to the pastor, as if they have the time and support necessary to be able to add this to their task list. However, "developing a program that focuses on "fixing" our clergy only is to miss the holistic nature of the church. First, it wrongly focuses blame on the clergy. Second, it is the laity who hold the greatest potential for leadership and direction in our churches. We have consistently underutilized the laity and their secular expertise in the church. Under the guise of not wanting burn them out, or have their work bleed over to the church,"[14] says Bishop Hagiya.

The good news is there is movement and a budding courage to begin addressing this systemic issue. Stopping the insanity, so to speak. In May of 2022, Pastor Lee Cummings addressed the gathered leaders of the Radiant Church Network in Kalamazoo. MI. In his opening remarks he declared "a new reformation is taking place." Cummings envisioned the Priesthood of All Believers as the embodiment of the future. He challenged current leaders to go first, starting with prayer at the center to open our minds, acknowledging that revival begins in God's own household. "We need a new order," he implored. "This time, let' be meticulous. Do this right."[15]

Summary - The clergy/lay leadership system is deeply rooted in our systems and psyche. We have created organizations with a single point of failure that do not reflect how the church was designed to be led. This is not the result of bad people or singular decisions, and changing this will be very hard work. However, the movement to do so has begun.

Chapter Five

What if? Communal Leadership

The pathway forward is in pursuing the *spoude*-type organization-building leadership in community – Clergy and lay leadership sharing this role. We have everything we need to take this step. Jesus left it for us in the form of the five-fold gifts expressed in Ephesians 4:11-12. "So Christ himself gave the apostles, the prophets the evangelists, the pastors and the teachers, to equip his people for works of service, so that the body of Christ may be built up." Yes, built up. The body of Christ is to be built up.

In this most approachable pathway, the split between clergy and lay leadership disappears within these gifts. Cummings envisioned this next step with the Radiant Network as he declared the "priesthood and systems have to be reconsidered." The priesthood of all believers has traditionally been applied to lay persons missional work in their homes, places of work, community and schools. A "When you leave this room you are the ministers" sign hanging in the sanctuary is a reminder of this identity. Or our priesthood is lived out serving in church work in the various teaching, worship leader, caregiving, or administrative roles. To assist in executional leadership. All necessary and helpful, and for many of us, the perfect place for and expression of our gifts.

But the organization-building leadership adaptations require an expanded vision for the role of lay leadership. One that creates room for those gifted and called to this leadership role. For the pastor has been gifted one of these five-fold gifts as a primary motivation and one as a primary communication style. Where do the others come from? This is the critical and missing role of the priesthood of all believers in current leadership systems.

There are those lay persons gifted and called to this ministry. Those willing to reorient their lives to give the time, attention, study and prayer to the admittedly hard task. Desirous to grow into Christlikeness through the refining fire of organization-building, status quo-defying leadership. Willing to join the clergy in the space where our vocational positions will be reduced, our membership rights relinquished, our successes and credentials returned as the gifts they are. In this space, our previous seniority, sacrifice and service are seen as irrelevant, offered on the alter of death and new life. We can become a trusted part of an organization-building leadership community. We can share the burden and the joy. Here, no one needs to be alone. It is not what Christ envisioned.

Practically, and not surprisingly, there are advantages to the quality of the work, as well. The image of Camelot and King Arthur's Round Table is useful in thinking about diverse gifts and perspectives working together as equals. It was not a table of noble knights gathered to be yes men to King Arthur. But by design, and despite rank, unique gifts and contrary views were brought to leadership questions. The knights traveled together in fully devoted lives while pursuing their shared mission together.

President Abraham Lincoln is famous for putting his political opponents on his cabinet when he was on his way to becoming as effective a President as we've known. This is a very upside down Kingdom-like paradox, seemingly foolish. But it taps into the power of the creator of all things. And for us in church leadership, we know it based on what Alan Hirsch, prolific author and foreseer of the missional 21st Church movement, has codified with the APEST.[16]

Apostle, Prophet, Evangelist, Shepherd, Teacher (APEST)

APEST is the very fabric of what it means to be a church. Its contrarian nature is built-in creating the tension that produces change and growth. This power is latent within the whole Church community. It is this power that the Holy Spirit activates to animate the Church. So what of leadership, then? "Leadership in light of APEST can be conceived as a 'Calling within a Calling'; it is a distinct task that entails leading and influencing the body of Christ, not just ministering." [17]

Lets try some re-imagination of church leadership. What if our organization-building leadership experiences became the most anticipated gatherings on our calendar? What if our communal discernment modeled the intersection of theology and practice that led to creativity and innovation in approach? What if our experience challenged and inspired us to invest time and resources to become better at our craft? What if it sparked ever-increasing generosity and humility within us? Is it possible we would schedule our vacations around our church leadership rhythms? What if our leadership experience became the inspiration to model our vocational organization's leadership approaches and structures?

Extend this! What if our church leadership experience and practices led to better organizations in our city? Jim Collins addresses this issue in his *Good to Great and Social Sectors*, specifically why business thinking is not the answer.

"Social sector organizations increasingly look to business for leadership models and talent, yet I suspect we will find more true leadership in the social sectors than the business sector... True leadership only exists if people follow when they have the freedom not to.... Indeed, perhaps tomorrow's great business leaders will come from the social sector, not the other way around." [18]

Not just the social sector, but the Church. We have all we need to do this. And we need to humbly pursue this re-imagined role and form of leadership. And while we have had this opportunity all along, it is imperative we embrace it now. For some things have unalterably changed, and will not change back. We will see why in Section II; For Such a Time as This.

Summary - While we may feel trapped by systems and identities, there is a way out. It is right in front of us and easily accessible. Look more deeply into APEST way of leading. There is a movement building around this as we reclaim the work we were created to do. Let's join in. In pursuing this, we also perform one of the functions of organization-building leadership: reimagining what is possible. There are reasons why we need to take this seriously, now.

Section II - For Such a Time as This. Why are these leadership adaptations not optional if we are to move forward?

"At the center of all this, Christ rules the church. The church, you see, is not peripheral to the world; the world is peripheral to the church. The church is Christ's body, in which he speaks and acts, by which he fills everything with his presence."

Paul's letter to the Ephesians 1: 19-23. The Message.

"And who knows but that you have come to your royal position for such a time as this?"

Esther 4:14b. TNIV

Overview

We are truly living in liminal space. It is unlike anytime in modern history. Irrevocable changes out of our control have conspired to create out current upheavals. But here we are, in a leadership role where the we have the unique opportunity to co-create a future that aligns with God desires for all people. Is the nascent Transformative City Network movement a part of this? And can those native to our current culture collaborate with those most challenged to navigate these waters? While these changes are hard, nature has given us a metaphor on how we can safely proceed. It is as the inchworm. There is no sure answer, but the inchworm models a pathway to discovery and discernment. Now is the time.

Act III

I've been described as pretty focused. Overly focused, even. The focus on faith development and these two Kingdom principles eventually led me to leave my Fortune 500 general management job to become an Executive Pastor at the very same local church. This journey is a crazy story itself, way too much for this book. However, there are a few things things I remember that were markers on the journey.

I loved my corporate job. The challenge, the global nature of it, the travel and the late nights with co-workers discovering new ways to make artificial flooring important in your life. I often hear vocational change stories as people leaving the evil secular world for the good sacred world. To be clear, that is not at all how I viewed my change, and 20 years later I know that it is not even a valid proposition. I hoped I had been following a vocational call in my life at the time, and only now can I confidently say that it was exactly that.

I was invited to be in lay church leadership early on for the wrong reasons. Initially I resisted. Not out of a sense of running from 'call', or anything. That came later. But I don't think I was on this Christian journey but for a year or two and was asked to consider being on some leadership team. Not sure which, I don't remember. My qualifications had to do with my experiences at my job. It seemed very odd to me. My only experience in moving into more responsibility at my job was after being prepared for such a role. This didn't feel right. So in looking for guidance I eventually ran across or was guided to this scripture. "Do not be hasty in the laying on of hands" (1 Timothy 5:22) was Paul's instruction when appointing elders. When I expressed reluctance at saying yes, I was assured being asked to do this administrative or temporal work was not an appointment to eldership. I didn't see the difference. Still don't. Who we are matters.

People encouraged me to go to seminary to be trained theologically, doctrinally and become ordained. A proper Pastor. It would give me credibility. A career. I remember saying I would be open to it if I could see how it would help, I suppose I still am. But it seemed to be taking me off course. The two things pastors are expected to be good at (preaching and pastoral care) are skills in which I had proven to be un-gifted. Practice did not make perfect. And believe me, I tried, as I thought that was what good Christians did. Plus the church already had pastors. A slew of them. The senior pastor was and is a gifted preacher and teacher. We had multiple care pastors and a whole herd of people who helped us care for one another. The one who most let me off the hook on this path was the senior pastor himself, the one who preached the Priesthood of all Believers. I cherish the partnerships I enjoyed (and continue to enjoy) with seminary-trained leaders throughout the years; but it was not for me then. So I moved forward sans seminary, sans ordination.

I was also exposed to the larger Church. A diverse and beautiful thing. A big tent, as I've heard it described. Denominational conferences, conferences with other denominations and non-denominations. I experienced the Church as part of our local community, in partnership with other churches. A year-long learning community about the externally-focused church exposed me to many new people and ideas are still an influence today, twenty years later.

I learned a lot. About people, about myself, about this organization called the Church. The local church taught me what it means to be a leader. I have had the highest of highs and the lowest of lows as result of this following this call. I believe leadership in the Church is the most demanding leadership role, and the finest crucible for formation into Christ-likeness. How can it not be? What other organization has as its head and founder Jesus Christ? And what does He lovingly but unrelentingly require?

Chapter Six

Liminal Space

Is it really such as time as this? Is all this reformation and deconstruction talk just an overreaction to our normal changes in generations? We've been through all this before, right?

Let's consider this thing called liminal space. Liminal is a word that picked up usage quite a bit in the last 30 years. The results of a Google Ngram viewer search on word usage return this phenomena.

Use over time for: liminal

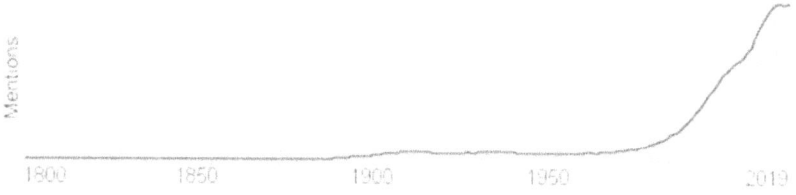

Apparently, we did not need this word for the 220 years previous. Not during the Civil War, World War I, the smallpox epidemic, the Great Depression, nor World War II. Incredibly difficult and challenging times.

50

Best described as "Not quite dead, not quite alive" liminal space is that in-between spot. We feel it in our leadership when we know what used to work doesn't, but what will work in the future has not yet been discovered. It is a very disorienting time. And it lasts far too long.

We could make the argument that the focus on liminality doesn't represent a response to a change of culture, but it is a 'fad' word we have adopted to describe our generational change experience. As Seth Godin pointed out on an episode of Cary Nieuhoff's leadership podcast, "recent history was all about the Boomers in charge, and now it is about the Boomer's decline."[19] So much like the word beatnik of the 1950's, speakeasies of the 1920's, or Secesh of the 1860's; it's just the word of our time. And if so, we can ride this out. The Church has made it through before, it'll be rough but we'll be fine. But to think that is our full reality today would be a big mistake.

We need to open our aperture and look at four drivers of change that affect us all, not just the generational cycle. There are two cycles that lead to predictable outcomes: the generational and church cycles. There are two others that lead to unpredictable outcomes: the transformational periods and transitional cycle. None of the four of these are controllable nor interruptible, which thankfully, only gives us the option of responding to them. Mike Regele's 1995 *Death of the Church* is the basis for the summary overviews below and an excellent resource for a deeper understanding.

Generational Cycle - Predictable

Regele asserts the generational cycles last about 80 years and is broken into 4 periods of about 20 years each. So in that 80 years we get back to where we were with some refinements based on two periods where society focuses inwardly, and two periods of a societal outward focus around a secular crisis. As history has shown, these are predictable and repeatable. We can see we are in period headed toward what Regele described as follows. "An emerging communitarian spirit to face social problems, the 80 year era culminates in secular crisis, a single ideal prevails over others, and new foundation for community building."[20] We are at an inflection point in this change cycle right now. We can feel it. It's pretty much all we talk about.

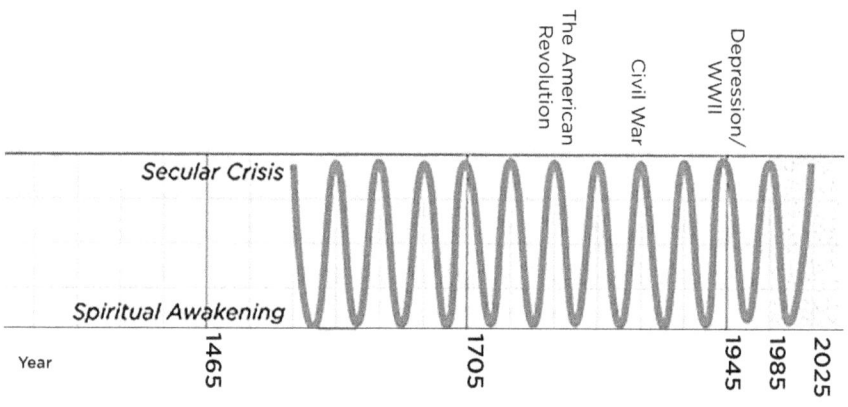

Generation Cycle as described by Mike Regele
image by Tom Nealley

Church Cycle - Predictable

The Church cycle is particularly relevant to us. This cycle has two periods that last about 40 years each and align with the generational cycles. They are the Doing Faith Period and the Experiencing Faith Period. The Experiencing Faith Period is an awakening period for the church, and where phrases like "relationship, not religion" resonate. The Doing Faith period results in the development of the external forms of the Church.

Today we are in the transition from Experiencing Faith to Doing Faith, a second inflection point.

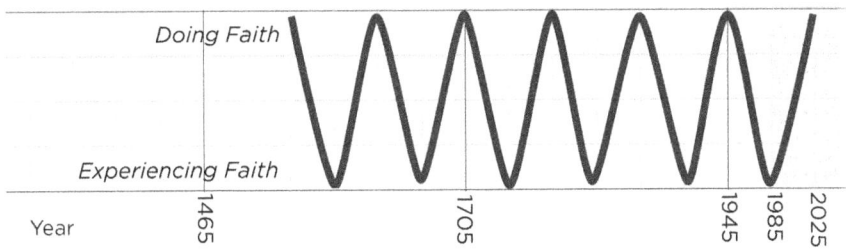

Church cycle as described by Mike Regele
image by Tom Nealley

The good news is we can look back at these predictable change cycles for some level of comfort. Regele points out that understanding the rhythm of the generational cycle and the church change cycle can help us avoid a lot of frustration as well as the sense of failure. It is human to vacillate between the periods and they actually create balance over long haul.[21]

However, if those two change cycles were all we were experiencing, then there would be no need for this book and its ultimate invitation. There is more going on. Eric Swanson[22] recently shared a similar insight with a cohort of Transformative City Network leaders. Highlighting well-known ministry leadership books, including his own, he said the underlying message is: "We've figured it out, so you don't have to. Just do what we've done, and you'll succeed like we've succeeded." He points out that this approach has worked for complicated problems like these cycles produce. And if this were still true, we could stay in our execution leadership lane and work on improvement. But he said this approach no longer serves. This was not a criticism of the books or the underlying message.

Both were right for such a time as that. But they are only partially helpful now. So why??

Transformational Period - Unpredictable

Regele describes a Transformational Period as a tidal wave where not only is the beach gone, but much inland is changed permanently, if not destroyed. The change produced by this tidal wave is chaotic. Assumptions about how things work are crushed, people and things are out of control and our best efforts to change it back to normal fail. Discomfort levels go through the roof and our values and belief systems are fundamentally challenged. Regele allowed that it is overwhelming to wrap our minds around such a notion.[23] We react and cry out for "Order, Order."

With hindsight we can name the Transformational Periods relevant to us today. Starting with the hunter-gatherer period to an agrarian-based socio-economic structure through to the industrial revolution and an industrial society. This industrial society built around nation-states has led to our current information-based society built around a global village. The United States was founded as an agrarian society, and was able to transition quickly to an industrial society as a young country growing through the 1800's. But how quickly our industrial prowess spawned this next period. Today we are right in the midst of a Transformational Period tidal wave.

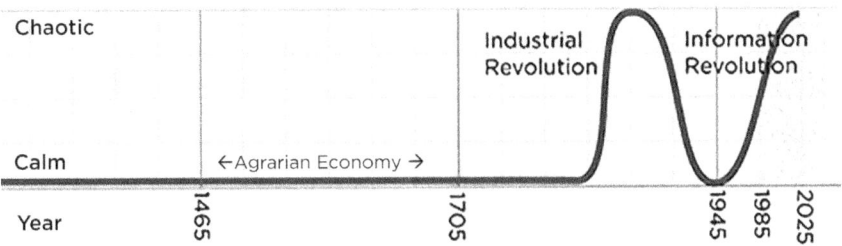

Transformational Periods as described by Mike Regele
image by Tom Nealley

Transitional Cycle - Unpredictable

In 2008 Phyllis Tickle picked up the story. In her book *The Great Emergence.* While not referencing the work of Regele, she identifies the very same reality which "has been slipping up on us for decades in the very much the same way spring slips upon us week by week every year."[24]

While acknowledging the Transformational wave crest we are experiencing, she focuses on the Transitional change wave as it accompanies the others. She confirms everything is right on time, as we could have expected.

Tickle quotes The Right Reverend Mark Dyer that "the only way to understand what is currently happening to us as 21st Century Christians in North America is first to understand that about every 500 years the Church feels compelled to hold a giant rummage sale. About every five hundred years the empowered structures of institutionalized Christianity, whatever they may be at that time, become an intolerable carapace that must be shattered in order that renewal and new growth may occur."[25] This is the Transitional cycle.

So let's go back the first 500 years from today to the Great Reformation then back another 500 to the Great Schism; then back up to Gregory the Great and the Monastics who "Saved Civilization" during the decline of the Roman Empire; and back another 500 to beginning of Christianity and Jesus Christ.

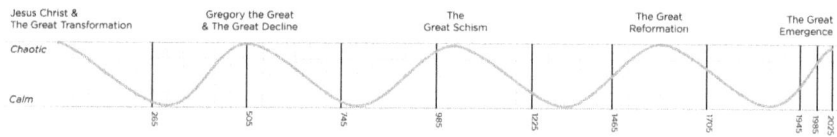

Transitional Cycles as described by Phyllis Tickle
image by Tom Nealley

Tickle points out that "no standing form of organized Christian faith has ever been destroyed by one of our millennial eruptions."[26] Humbled, yes. And out of each period arose new forms, and overall Christianity spread and grew. But then that is the gospel, is it not?

The rummage sale metaphor holds great hope for us if we can embrace our role in this time and place; that we are not in control but participating in something truly historic that the writers of the year 3000 will name the Great "something." Tickle proposed the name the Great Emergence; for we really don't know. But we don't get to name it. Only those that see the fruits of God's work through us and the next few generations will name this period of the Transitional Cycle.

Amplification - unknown and unknowable

Regele then picks up on the concept of amplification. Think, again, of the ocean. Sometimes waves cancel each other out. When two waves from different sources come together, one in trough and one cresting, the result can be a surprisingly placid outcome. If we were in a boat at that very point in time, we might not even notice. Or we wonder why that wave coming our way a few seconds ago didn't seem to affect us. We were bracing for some rocking. But it wasn't so bad.

Alternately when two waves come together and they are both cresting, we get the amplified excitement of the energy exploding into large crashes, sprays of water and an increase of speed and power. We find ourselves in the water, the boat crashed upon the shore, wondering what just happened!

In both cases two waves came together in the same time and place—it was their inflection points that made the difference. So what if four waves are coming at our boat, cresting at the same time? Is the ensuing reaction an amplification of two times more, four times, some logarithmic exponential explosion? Frankly, other than the fact that there will be remarkable turbulence, the rest is unknown and even unknowable.

This summarizes our plight today. Never before have we lived in such a time where all four cycles are in transition, all inflecting, and all cresting. There is no canceling out for us. The diagram on the following page depicts why we are in liminal space and moving into unknown and unknowable territory.

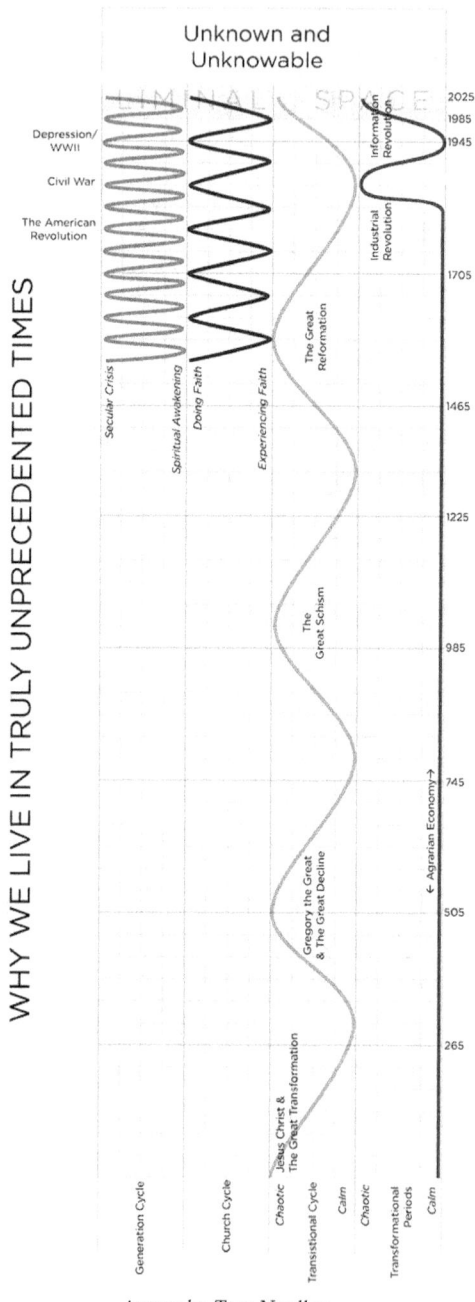

image by Tom Nealley

So is it really such a time as this, or just hyperbole? Are we really in true liminal space? More than ever, the evidence suggests it is real. More than ever. Ooph.

Our leadership skills and vision must adapt to navigate this reality. We must reclaim the organization-building Leadership function to not merely survive, but more importantly, to create the future in partnership with the Holy Spirit.

Summary - We are truly living in liminal space. It is unlike any time in modern history, and we are not able to predict the future, nor control the factors that are causing the upheaval in society and in our beloved Church. We can now be confident that what we are experiencing is not caused by us, just as we did not choose to be born when we were. The Spirit is reforming Christ's Church, and we don't get to live in one of the calm eras of our Christian forms and expressions. This is both our problem to navigate and opportunity to innovate.

Chapter Seven

The Inchworm

As leaders we may well have tried to address these realities in some fashion. In which case we have experienced the power of the status quo resisting even our initial efforts; and the sheer effort it takes to persevere is overwhelmed by our day to day duties. Or perhaps, more insidiously, realizing what started out as a promising change initiative is, within a few months, dissolved in a sea of confusion and frustration. So where might we turn?

Perhaps the created order has something to offer. There are reality lessons all around us in nature. Not insisting to be heard, but available 24/7 to remind us of the deepest truths. And if we are open, to guide our thinking. Consider the almost invisible inchworm and its lessons for the organization-building leadership function as a natural metaphor for movement. Especially given we are called to lead change within the church, and all the complexities that brings.

The Inchworm metaphor for communal leadership

A research project identified the unique characteristics of the inchworm to inspire innovation in mobility technology design.[27] The final report offered these insights. "The inchworm is capable of maneuvering in extremely small spaces, can do so in arbitrary orientations to gravity and can withstand substantial external forces attempting to diverge it from its intended course. It can do these things because its mobility system is governed by a simple rule: 'Never let go of what you are holding until you are holding something else.'

The inchworm strategy is deceptively simple yet extraordinarily powerful. Having an elongated body with many small footpads placed at either end, the inchworm's mode of locomotion is to firmly attach the rear portion of its body to a surface via its footpads, then extend the remainder of its body forward. Next, the inchworm attaches the front part of its body to a surface and brings the rear up to meet the front. In this way, the inchworm is able to move forward while at the same time, always staying grounded.

Inchworm motion
image by Alexander Ferworn and Deborah Stacey

This type of movement is particularly suited to unstructured or even hostile environments. As an inchworm moves forward it has the opportunity to sense what is in front of it without having to commit to a surface that might reveal itself to be unsafe or unsteady. At the same time, the system's low silhouette and center of gravity provide the animal with a high degree of stability."

As we deal with our unstructured 21st Century context, this is a profound metaphor. We are headed into the unknown and unknowable. Given our leadership triple challenge of selectively forgetting the past, managing what already exists, while simultaneously creating the future; this metaphor offers a pathway forward. It highlights the most creative tension I think we have going for us as organization-building leaders. For the inchworm is all about movement. There is no such thing as staying still. We are called into the culture, into the huge challenges we face as a society.

Older leaders

However, many of us who hold position and authority are trained for a world that no longer exists. We are understanding the need for change, but feel unequipped or fearful of leading into it, or are just plain tired. It's been a good run, but we don't have the energy or health to do this new work. The inchworm shows we have a role in supporting the reforming movement. It is holding onto what we know with the important back pads until it is time to move the whole body, until we've discovered the next step. Then we release, making it OK, for the whole body to move on the path forward.

Alternatively, some of us 'old guard' leaders are called, willing and able to be on the front pads of the inchworm. And while that may be so, we need to realize we are foreigners in another's land. If we are there, it must be with humility to learn from younger leaders who are native to the information revolution culture. It is not our role to train up the younger leaders to be like us. For we have an even more important role. We have something invalauble to offer to the creators of the future.

Think of Pixar movies, like Toy Story (1, 2, 3, 4), Cars (1, 2, 3) and eighteen others, all executed with amazing technology. This approach to movie-making was the next stable foothold for the motion picture industry as technology threatened the former ways of movie creation. And we picture rooms and buildings full of young people doing this miraculous new and wonderful work using computers, animation and inventing whatever tools were needed when they did not otherwise exist. When Ed Catmull, the President of Pixar was asked about this, and how the young people could come up with such captivating stories he had a remarkable answer. Paraphrasing he said, "Oh no. They don't write the stories. They have not lived life to see the whole way through. The ones with the imagination and creativity to tell compelling stories are over 55. They are coming into the most creative part of their lives. They keep the young people executing the production of the movie connected to the story."[28] Preach it and Amen.

Younger Leaders

Younger leaders are anxious to move forward. Harness the technology, create what needs to be created and ground themselves in what they understand to be the foundations of their faith. They are "all in" on this new work. It is their future reality for the next forty or so years. They don't have the option to 'ride it out'. Writers are now calling them the pioneers as contrasted to the settlers harkening back to another time of discovery. They bring a zeal to this work, having zero interest in maintaining the status quo.

Still, they need to be equipped in organization-building leadership skills, while at the same time develop compassion for what we might consider the "stuck" older leaders. For is it possible we older leaders are also critical to the reformation? While our younger leaders are catalyzing and sustaining working relationships that will continue to power this change over the next thirty years, we need the older leaders' vision, imagination, resources, influence, and long-standing networks and relationships to move the body forward. We are inter-dependent.

Our best fighting chance for movement into this unknown and unknowable territory is as the inchworm. Where the whole body contributes as it uniquely must.

Summary: The inchworm is able to move, even if slowly, in the unknown and unknowable. Its ability to explore new options while holding onto what is known is the most hopeful description of how we, as the church body, can move forward. The metaphor shows how both those that are slow to change and those that are eager to change can help one another. Beyond help one another, collaborate so that the entire body safely moves forward.

Chapter Eight

Transformational City Networks

We trust God is working through us to point His way into the unknown and unknowable. Those of us that are on the front pads of the inchworm, looking for a safe landing spot, have discovered one of the movements. Since the 1970's, the nascent Transformative City Network approach to renewal has emerged. It has all the hallmarks of what Regele believed would be present at this time in history and it is animated by distributed impact network leadership systems.

Eric Swanson is a catalyst within this movement, and been connecting, equipping and mentoring these networks throughout the world. Swanson points to the mid 1970's as the early indicators of the movement. One of the many pioneers of the time was Ray Bakke (for whom the Bakke Graduate University is named), who worked diligently to advance leadership globally. Swanson was a great friend and mentee of Bakke, and is a graduate of the university.

In sharing the history, Swanson said an early distinction the movement made was with regards to revival in a city. He says the best way to think of it is railroad tracks. "Praying and waiting" for God to bring revival apart from the church can be visualized as one of the rails of the track. On this rail, God gives us a momentary glimpse of what could be. But this one rail alone is not sufficient, or our society would look more like the Kingdom. It needs the second rail, which engages the Church (as people and institution) and provides structures to sustain the work into future generations. This is the "obey and go" mission rail; where it is the Church's role to bring unity and social change at increasingly greater and broader levels. Both rails are necessary for this metaphorical train to move. The Transformative City Network is the emerging second rail, bringing sustaining structure to the power of revival.

At the network's core is the church's relationship to all of society. Rather than church being a sector of society like business, arts and media, social service, government, education, health-care and others, siloed from one another, each other doing its own thing—what if it were something else? What if the Church was the unifying body that brought the sectors together for the good of all in the city? What if the desires of the Church and the desires of the city are in many cases the exact same – that the people are safe, healthy, joyous, and thriving? What if they worked together with the objective of decreasing certain statistics to 0% of the population? And what if there was an organization that could convene the one Church to unite and mobilize it to serve this greater good, without each local church expression losing its unique traditions and practices?

This is the Social Innovation, as defined by Phil McKinney, that is occurring within the city with local church leaders. There are excellent resources to learn about this movement.[29] Swanson claims it is still very early in its formation. "Day One," as he put it. But the essence of these organizations captures much of how the Church will be influential and lead change in the 21st Century. It is a safe landing spot for the future.

This visual summarizes the theology and practice of how Transformative City Networks operate with a city, or any geography that shares a common cause for which they want to see change. The networks are centered where the three circles overlap. There are hundreds of varying types of Transformative City Network convening organizations being formed–each different in approach due to context, but united in cause. The Shalom of the City.

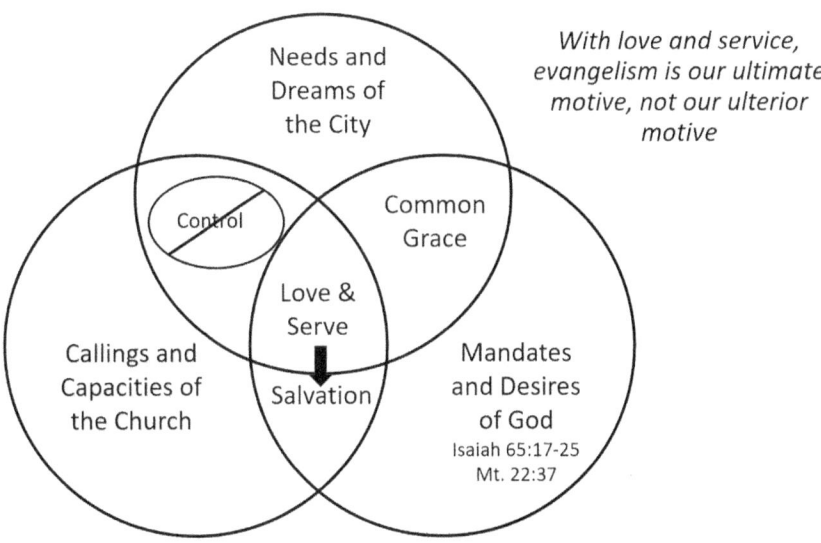

Venn diagram on discovering common ground in city transformation.
image by Eric Swanson

The Venn diagram helps us see the common ground where faithful collaboration can occur with the three key entities at play.[30] Let's take a quick look at each and how they have informed the Transformative City Network movement.

Needs and Dreams of the City.

Every city has needs and problems to be addressed, as well as hopes and dreams for the people of the city, and for the reputation of the city, itself. Transformational City Network leaders ask the leaders of the sectors what exactly these needs and aspirations are. What barriers and obstacles are they facing? They listen on behalf of the Church.[31] The leaders describe exactly the kind of city each of us would love to live in. Not surprisingly, they focus on physical and material problems rather than spiritual ones. But they clearly also describe the common ground between government and church leaders.

Mandates and Desires of God.

This represents God's vision for a healthy city. When God envisioned building a city from scratch (Isaiah 65:17-25), he created blueprint of the physical, social, economic aspects of a healthy city.[32]

Calling and Capacity of the Church.

While each local church may have differing capacity, we all share a common calling. "...God has given to his people the responsibility and privilege of defending the powerless and speaking up for those without a voice in our communities–the poor, widows, orphans, single moms, prisoners, immigrants, elderly, sick, and disabled."[33]

The Intersections of these entities is where we gain insight.

Common Grace

This is when the mandates and desires of God overlaps with the needs and dreams of the city, apart from the church. It includes things like schools, streetlights, sewers, roads and police and fire protection as examples. Though the church does care about these things when they are missing, it is outside of our call to provide them. As Swanson points out, "Martin Luther King defined the role of the church in this regard: "The church is neither servant of the city nor master of the city but the conscience of the city."[34]

Control

Control is the intersection between the city and the church, apart from the will of God. It represents where one entity attempts to exert power over the other. In every instance of this playing out it "has failed to lead to a sustained impact for the gospel and has not furthered the growth and expansion of the kingdom."[35] This is an area where it is not fruitful for leaders of any entity to enter.

Salvation

This is when the calling and capacity of the church and the mandates and desires of God overlap for the good of the city. What is interesting about this space is that "no one in the city is necessarily asking to be saved... at least in spiritual sense."[36] This informs how we approach our calling, as summed up by the phrase in the upper right of the diagram, "with love and service, evangelism is our ultimate motive, not our ulterior motive."

Love and Serve

The center is the sweet spot where all the entities come to-gether in common agreement. As the church takes the posture of love and service, this agreement transcends disagreement. "Cities resist being 'reached,' but they love being served, loved and blessed."[37] From the deep relationships formed in meaningful service with people from all sectors of the city we build bridges to the conversations where the good news of salvation is invited.

Convening Organizations

There have been and continue to be church-based and non-profit organizations formed to facilitate this movement. These organizations convene the leaders of the sectors of the city for fruitful collaboration with the church and one another. They also convene and equip church leaders to unite the witness of the church to the other sectors.

An example of how this manifests practically is For Richmond, of Richmond, Va. When the Richmond Public Schools (RPS) had a family crisis the public safety net could not accommodate, RPS called For Richmond looking for immediate relief. Because of the relationship with 220 churches, For Richmond knew immediately who could help and within minutes were able to tell RPS "yes." The relief from RPS staff was palpable. From there, For Richmond was able to convene a coalition of four churches to provide ongoing recovery support for the family. A key tenet of these organizations is the local church gets the credit for coming through in partnership with RPS. It is a local church who supplied what was needed, who For Richmond told RPS was the trusted partner. For Richmond was merely the conduit, in the background doing what neither the family, RPS, or the churches by themselves could do on their own.

Leaders of these organizations are many times former local church leaders with a passion for this work. These leaders are in the same boat as local church leaders. Together we are in the process of forming these nascent convening organizations, building platforms and networks to facilitate the work of the Church. It is clear we all need to transcend our past experiences in executional leadership to organization-building leadership functions, for indeed that is the role. As we do so, it is apparent that our local church leaders also become skilled in these organization-building leadership skills. Especially as they relate to leading a network within a network. For we are all in this together.

Summary: an emerging outcome of The Great Emergence, as Phyllis Tickle called it, is the City Transformation Network. The organization's work is to unify the church and convene the leaders of all sectors to work on behalf of the good of the city. This movement to the collaborative church demands new organization-building leadership skills for the network leaders and church leaders who desire to participate. This intersection of social and institutional innovation is why we must make these leadership adaptations. For such a time as this.

Chapter Nine

Communal Leadership across Generations

As we apply the inchworm metaphor to help us navigate the unknown and unknowable terrain of the future, we will turn our focus on the generational cycle, and the unique implications it has for this time. When Regele outlined the challenge we were facing, he offered up a very concrete approach in the *Death of the Church*. That was to name, envision and claim the role that each of the generational life stages have in creating the 21st Century Church.[38] For such a time as this.

For this framework to provide any value, reclaiming our organization-building leadership functions is mandatory. Since the book was written in 1995, the generational perspective needs to be updated to 2023. Having done so, the framework, then, is as follows:

Those over age 45. Leaders in this age range role are to embrace and model organization-building leadership where we currently have authority and power. This includes, most importantly, the imagination of a new Kingdom-based story of reality; the grand vision of life. Additionally, this cohort has most financial resources and are to release them to the work of others. Over the next 20 years will be the greatest wealth transfer in history as assets are bequeathed.[39] How those are stewarded for Kingdom purposes will be of great importance. Once the vision has been reimagined, resources directed, there is a third role. Sharing and enabling leadership with others. Bill Drayton of ASHOKA says it this way when engaging younger leaders: "Ask what they think they can do to solve the problem. Give them time and space as they self-organize and get out of the way."[40]

Age 25 - 44. This is who will provide the creativity and exe-cutional leadership needed to put together the new structures of Church that allow the envisioned Church to practically work. This cohort will work as the head of the inchworm, experimenting, trying, learning. They will sense what is ahead, determine that which is steady, refine and codify the next step for the Church. They will work in partnership with those that are holding onto what we know in order to move the whole body to its new destination.

Ages 7 - 24. They will carry the new church forward as part of our DNA. Through participation in the work of the new structures, the cohort will grow into disciples of Christ in the envisioned way, solidifying the Church and its role in society. This will sustain the patient work of the Holy Spirit into the future, ensuring the legacy of the previous generations.

Ages under 6 will enjoy the fruits of the renewed Church. They will be the first to enjoy the period of stability on the other side of the liminal space. As we are called to deal with the chaos of the amplification of the four cycles in transition, they will begin to live in the calm parts of the various cycles. For that will be their time.

This movement has already begun and we are feeling its effects. Our opportunity is to embrace this framework versus resist the inevitable. We can re-frame any challenges we feel from our generational differences as opportunities for collaboration.

Our current leadership transition.

In *The New Copernicans,* David John Seel outlines the challenge. Writing in 2018 about our liminal space and journey into the unknown and unknowable, Seel asserts: "...they are the best harbor pilots to navigate these waters. It is for this reason that millennial New Copernicans are the hope of the church. It is difficult for a parent to give the keys to the car to their teenage driver. It is equally difficult for a child to take away the keys from an aging parent. These kinds of transitions are difficult but often necessary. The transition of leadership to emerging millennial church leaders is vital for the evangelical church."[41] While Seel was writing to the evangelical church, the same sentiments and reality are present for all churches. Indeed, for any institution that hopes to have influence in the remainder of the 21st Century.

Barna's[42] research helps bring some additional insight to what has changed. As the emerging leaders need to have compassion for what they perceive as "stuckness" in us older leaders, we older ones have the same challenge to honor their reality.

"Through our careful listening, we've come to hold several core convictions about these young adult generations, whom we call Millenials and Gen Z.

- They are deeply misunderstood by older generations of Christian leaders.

- They are coming of age in a radically different context, one that could be described as chaotic.

- Their skepticism is giving way to indifference - a much more intractable problem.

- They are hungry to see courageous leaders in all facets of society.

- This generation doesn't just want to know that Christianity is true, they want to know that it is good.

They are desperately in need of a wise, compassionate, listening ear - and we are desperately in need of their partnership as we look to the Church's future."[43]

Seth Godin was quoted earlier as part of Carey Niehouf's podcast. In the same interview when asked if he saw younger people as more isolated and bitter, Seth's response was "Did you say the word bitter? I would like to say I am seeing the opposite. The headlines and the people with traffic on social media are trolls, and these are people who are willing to trade self-respect for attention, and we can ignore them if we want. But the human beings I am volunteering with on the Carbon Almanac, the people who I interact with, my friend in Italy who is dealing with a health problem, the folks who I know who just graduated from medical school, the kids who are coming up; I am seeing the opposite. I am seeing a true desire, not for scale, but for quality. Not just quality in what kind of clothes I am going to wear. But quality in, what is my life going to be like? What are my choices? If I am going to be next to somebody, who do I want to be next to?.... Most people are looking for possibility."[44]

Organization-building leadership functions are necessary to imagine that possibility and embrace the roles of the generations, the differing world views, the contrarian nature of perspectives. See these differences as assets to be released into the mission of the church. This work transcends the day to day church work and is the work of the Church today.

Summary: Due to the amplification effect of the four cycles and the introduction of the information reformation upon us, even the generational cycle has taken on new dimensions.

The transition feels riskier and more challenging than previous times for those of us that have been through it. But there is a pathway we can apply to give us the necessary guidance through envisioning the roles of each of the generations in our shared reformation work. We can move from competition between generations to collaboration within; modeling a way forward for all to see.

Section III - Redeeming Measurement. Can we reframe data and measures for learning to support our leadership adaptations?

Yearning for a new way will not produce it. Only ending the old way can do that.

You cannot hold onto the old, all the while declaring you want something new.

The old will defy the new;

The old will deny the new;

The old will decry the new.

There is only one way to bring in the new. You must make room for it.

Neale Donald Walsch

Overview

Measurement can be a tough subject in church leadership circles. Mainly because we have not even begun to tap into it's potential for supporting the changing of the status quo. Understanding and deploying measurement in a healthy learning manner will be mandatory. Additionally, our 21st Century Information Revolution has brought a new resource to the table to help provide insights we could not otherwise uncover, data. How we have used measurement and data in the 20th Century will not be helpful in the 21st. Fortunately there are movements and people deeply dedicated to providing the new perspectives. However, we will need new tools to support our organization-building leadership functions.

Act IV

For fourteen years I was in executive pastor-type roles at two churches. Seven years each. In between, I was president of a small building materials company. Which is not insignificant. Because that did not work out. Not because of lack of skills or competence; but lack of desire. I thought my church vocational work was done after my first church stint and I would bring my newfound leadership skills to a new environment. However, there is a responsibility to the people, the many stakeholders and the organization's goals as president. And in exchange for the various perks that come with it, fealty is expected; no, required. After hours, if there is such a thing, would be to learn more about the new industry, the people, what is unseen but influential nonetheless. It was then I realized: My heart, my passion, was with the local church and I would not stop thinking about it, reading about it, talking with friends about it. It was perhaps here my call asserted itself as love of the local church leaders and our plight. That was to be my focus. Not surprisingly, the owner of the company had come to the same conclusion, so we parted ways. Before I knew it, I was at the second church.

While the first church was in a historically Christian area, the second was far from it. A rapidly growing area with a diverse population, the Christian faith and its practices were well outside of the routine of most people. The church was diligent in exploring and experimenting with new ways to connect with people in this reality. Within the denomination, a national church consultant shared we were "...one of the most creative he was connected to. Pioneering and most cutting edge in discovering forms, rituals and rhythms." So, as you might expect, that is when the status quo went on the offensive. While creative and pioneering sounds wonderful to some people, to others, not so much. Conflict began to arise as the tension became apparent. Even the regional denominational authorities began to question the value of this work. Should we be investing high capacity leadership time and resources towards these new initiatives? Why don't you guys get back down to the business of growing our worship attendance? We discussed this openly within church and denominational leadership, and worked to bridge the gap. Our consultant encouraged us to see this institutional innovation as important work, declaring it "necessary for the larger denomination to see how to navigate this" inevitable tension. And it is in this space, I had a dream. Literally.

It was here that the seeds of measurement, and visualization began to take hold. It was clear we were struggling to apply the measures and assumptions of this church's first thirty years to what was emerging. Not that anyone was doing anything wrong, we just didn't have an alternative way to think. The dream was of a visualization I thought would be helpful in bringing a new and useful perspective to leadership and the congregation. (Looking back I can see the seeds of the dream were planted in 2003 and 2006 in the books *The Shaping of Things to Come* and *The Forgotten Ways* by Alan Hirsch.) It meant to tell a new story. Not only where we have been, for that founding story was a critical part of our identity, but of where we might be going. I drew it out. October 2013.

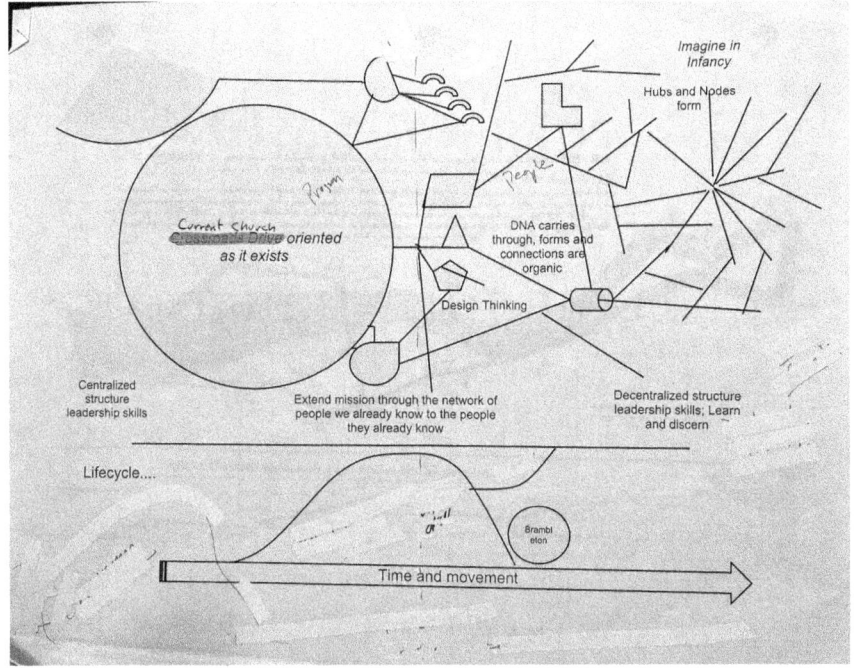

Current Church oriented as it exists

Program

People

Imagine in Infancy

Hubs and Nodes form

DNA carries through, forms and connections are organic

Design Thinking

Centralized structure leadership skills

Extend mission through the network of people we already know to the people they already know

Decentralized structure leadership skills; Learn and discern

Lifecycle....

Bramble ton

Time and movement

While this back of the napkin drawing was clearly rough, it was helpful to some leaders to re-frame their perspective and started new, more fruitful conversations. But it was tremendously flawed as it is static. For the story is multidimensional, dynamic and can only unfold over time. While this snapshot in time was interesting, it was inadequate. I envisioned this story being told over the 30 years of existence of the local church and it morphing into the pioneering work of today. I wanted to show that the new expressions of church were a normal extension of who we already were, not a cancer threatening to kill us.

So I went off to figure out how to do this. I knew the data tools and technology existed to create visualizations and bring new insights and new stories because I had used these types of tools in my other work. Surely someone had figured out these tools for Church leaders. Right? Right?

Chapter Ten

Tools for Change

As we embrace the function of organization-building leadership practices to navigate this unknown and unknowable terrain, we have to turn our attention to the tools we need to make our work possible. Tools we need and deserve. The first tool we are going to look at is measurement. Right alongside is its closest friend, data.

We can already feel the tension rise. "Not data and numbers!" Even if we suspect they are useful, we hear the refrains echoing throughout the cathedrals in our heads. *Unspiritual, unspiritual.* We are people, not numbers. What we do cannot be measured. That's religion, we are about relationships.

And there is a good reason behind this response. A reason we need to address.

We can't say numbers don't have value. They certainly do. The Bible is rife with them. They provide the power behind the three tellings of the feeding of the five thousand. Paraphrase the story without the numbers and it loses its miraculousness, its mystery. It's kinda boring. So they had a picnic. It would not have led to: "After the people saw the sign Jesus performed, they began to say. 'Surely this is the Prophet who is to come into the world'".[45] There is book called Numbers. It's there, even if not accessed much.

We've had numbers in front of us for years. It's how we talk about ourselves. We've been counting for years. Numbers provide clarity, help us understand and see movement and change. They reveal what is happening.

Actually, despite our protests, we overvalue them and allow them to define our identity. That is part of the power, I suspect. Worship attendance and dollars are things we are normally in tune with. In fact, we can pretty quickly recount them in any gathering with other church leaders. When they are rising, we sleep well and feel satisfied. When they are declining, not so much. We betray their importance to us when we insist they are not important to us. And improving these measures are often the focus of meetings, financial and human resource allocation, as well as training and consulting.

Certain numerical standards have provided useful services. Until the 21st Century, with its upheavals and liminal space. The information age and technology brought about something new with data. Something we are all inundated with now: analytics and algorithms that have changed how we live and relate to one another and the world. That have changed how people see and behave, obsoleting our standards. We think they have obsoleted us. Nope, just the standards.

Are your favorite sports teams run differently as result of data mining? Do managers and coaches have new tools at their disposal to help make decisions? You bet. Is there a culture clash within sports about the value and use of analytics? Absolutely. It can be used for good. And it can be used for bad.

This is where the fear comes in. As an example, from an article in the NY times in 2021 regarding world class runners:

"Johnson told The Oregonian that the use of those scans and body fat percentages meant that his judgments of athletes' weights weren't based on appearances but on data.

'When we get the numbers from our DEXA scans, we have an Excel spreadsheet that we can plug the numbers into, hit a button and it gives us a starting value for a training program,' he said. He added, 'Track is nothing but numbers. A good mathematician probably could be a good track coach.' And he explained that the DEXA scans were helpful for that 'nothing but numbers' approach. "That's one thing the DEXA scan helps us do," he told The Oregonian. "It takes our personal opinions out of it.'"[46]

So if this is what collecting data and measures is, then as a church leader, no thanks.

One window into the minds of millions is Anna, who has started a gathering to pray for the city in a local church. They have had one meeting so far. The executive director asked her how she was going to know if the gathering was successful: What were the measures? What did success look like? This, of course, induced panic. Isn't having a prayer meeting enough, Anna thought? All the alarm bells fired. There were not enough people here. Others must think this is a waste of time. It won't be big enough... oh my gosh, how will we grow this, for that must be what matters, right? Anna reached out for help with this invitation:

"I'm going to be honest, I'm not sure how I feel about gathering data as I am afraid how that would impact the team who are behind this."

Fear. Data, measures, numbers = fear. They will hurt people.

However, the underlying issue was the assumption Anna made regarding the measure. It has to be about people attending since that is all we do. We count. The obsolete standard.

"Measuring the wrong thing is worse than measuring nothing at all." is a wise quote from Seth Godin.

As we move into the cloud of the 21st Century we must be careful we do not carry the 20th Century measures forward with us as our guide. It will only give power to the status quo.

If, as organization-building leaders, we are to selectively forget the past, optimize the present and create the future simultaneously, then the power of measures is our best friend.

Measures, particularity of movement toward the changes we desire to see, is our number one lever to change our mindsets and culture. It is these measures, these new data points, that will interrupt the ladder of inference before we quickly ascend to our predictable conclusions and actions.

The very first place we must apply this new lever is in planning. The strategic planning process of the 20th Century no longer serves us well.

Planning

Strategic planning was popularized in the industrial age where the problems were complicated, but could be solved. Strategic planning is a great linear process that assumes we know what to do. It is an exercise of control. Through good research, due diligence, excellent understanding of the organization's unique strategic levers, clever tactics and execution, organizations can define and then accomplish their goals. The weak link in the planning process today, the one that is breaking down, is that our strengths are the result of serving a world that is gone. We end up unintentionally doubling down on what is not required. The planning process as outlined, ensures that. It's a devious trap. But we are in liminal space.

When we mention strategic planning many will point to the influence of Peter Drucker in introducing this practice. Ponder, then, this quote from Drucker: "Planning is actually incompatible with entrepreneurial society and economy. Planning is the kiss of death of entrepreneurship."[47] Our current environment, such a time as this, requires a new approach.

There are many fine strategic planning resources for church leaders. We've no doubt tried lots of them. These books, tools and facilitators do a great job of preparing leaders for the strategic planning retreat. And we go to the mountains for a night (or three)...

For our purposes we are going to look at this one page process. It is one of Eric Swanson's "how to strategically plan" gems that he presents to many church leaders. Eric is a master of reading up on a subject and distilling it to its essence. He then creates tools for church leaders to use. It really is a gift. We don't have to read strategic planning books because he boiled it down to seven pages with this graphic.

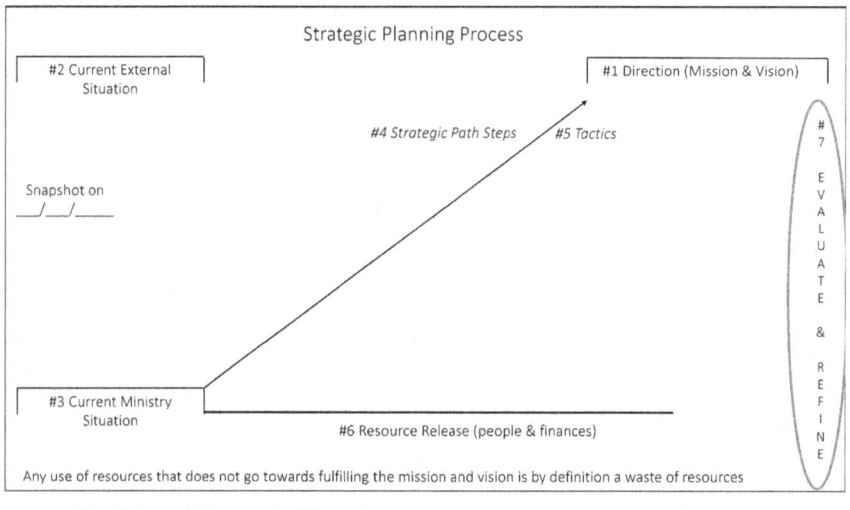

Traditional Strategic Planning process - measurement as final step
image by Eric Swanson

Note that measurement is step seven. And every strategic planning process ends with a phrase that basically says "Measure the results and adjust your plan accordingly."

And we know, at this point in the strategic planning weekend retreat, that this direction sounds just great. We are tired, having already blown our minds debating the difference between mission and vision and purpose and strategies and tactics and objectives and goals and actions. With our new vision statement, we did our best to align approaches and actions. We feel better as a group and lament that we don't get together like this more often. But as messy as the process is, the result is a step forward. A better plan than when we started. And at least for that weekend, we know the why behind the what! Simon Sinek would be pleased.

We celebrate and table the 'measure the results and adjust your plan accordingly' action step to later. Once we have the other stuff in place. For we are confident it will work, so the measuring is really.. optional. Besides, if we got that far during the weekend, our planning resources include sentences like "There are always ways to measure. The measurement may involve some creativity" do not sound like recipes for success. For as much effort was put into the "how to" of steps one through six, little has been put into figuring out 'how to' do step seven. So, quite right. It's easy to put off. Forever.

Even more fundamentally, it is asking us to make a culture shift that rarely any of the first six steps anticipate. Really, we have no idea how to do the seventh step to begin with, let alone make it part of the daily, weekly and monthly rhythms of our leadership.

However, our liminal context invites us to rearrange the steps in a way that makes sense for the current environment: what Swanson calls strategic pathing. A process that does not assume we know what to do, but does assume we are in touch with the deep call on our communal lives as an organization. This is our new path forward.

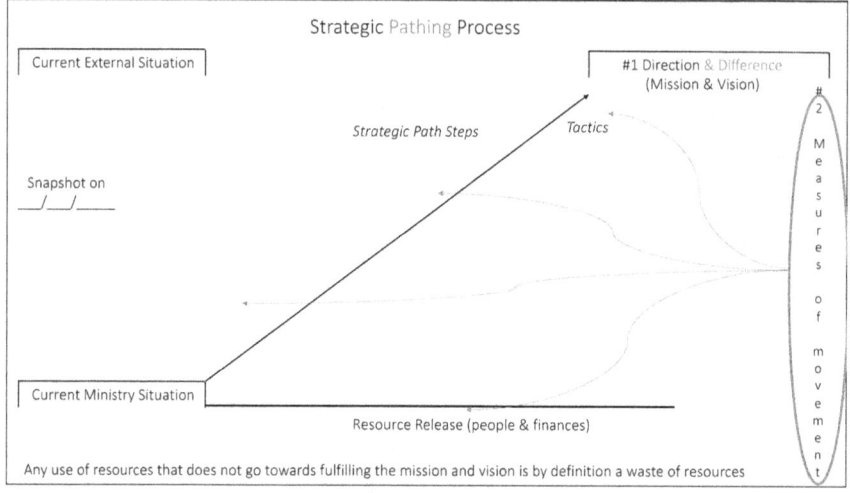

Adapting Strategic Planning Pathway for liminal space. Measurement at the beginning.
image by Eric Swanson, adapted by Tom Nealley

Summarizing the changed process, the sort of upside down or backwards approach would be 1) articulate what difference we are to make in the world and 2) determine how we would know if it was happening, both within and outside of our organization. We would then reorder the remaining. Who do we need to be in the future to effect these changes? Who are we today? What might have to die, even though it is not yet dead? How do we need to change? In which new areas might we need to become more skilled? What resources are available to help us? What might we need to learn?

We can redeem measures by moving them from an ignored afterthought to the powerful enemy of the deadly status quo. By keeping the measures, not the plan, in front, we are kickstarting a reflective conversational loop that will guide us through unknowing.

Summary: Measurement is an important tool in our leadership toolbox and is the most effective way to lead change in organization-building. This tool is not one that has been widely employed in church leadership in a healthy manner, but it can be redeemed. And as we lead into the unknown, it is mandatory that we elevate this tool to the front of our discussion about the future to provide the appropriate guidance.

Chapter Eleven

The World of Data

Before we get into more detail about measurement in the Church world, let's take a look out the window to what has happened in the transformational period called the information reformation. To give us a point of comparison it was 1455 when Johannes Gutenberg published the Bible as the first book ever printed on a press with movable type, and that technological advancement outside of the church is what fueled its reformation in the coming century. Our transitional cycle said we were ripe for this to happen again. The technological innovation fueled what wanted to happen anyway. And it did.

Over the last few thousand years, we have learned much about two very important resources we deploy and steward towards our common work and goals: people and money. They are integrated into all we do. We view stewarding these resources as necessary and good ministry.

The 21st century brings us another resource. We are just beginning to understand the value. We've only had 25 years with this resource; since 1996 when digital data storage became more cost-effective than paper. Leaders everywhere are still learning how to use and integrate it. This resource is data.

Using data as a resource is still an emerging capability in every organization. The technological innovation of the 21st Century has spurred this change, and we feel it every day. Clear examples are the Amazon shopping experience; any physical fitness app or tool that provides information about our health, wellness, and sleep recovery at a glance; and the GPS that routes us around an accident ahead. We can find out about anything in less than one second on Google search, and algorithms do the work of discerning what you want to see in your social media feeds. The recent release of Chat GTP has spurred the latest upheaval.

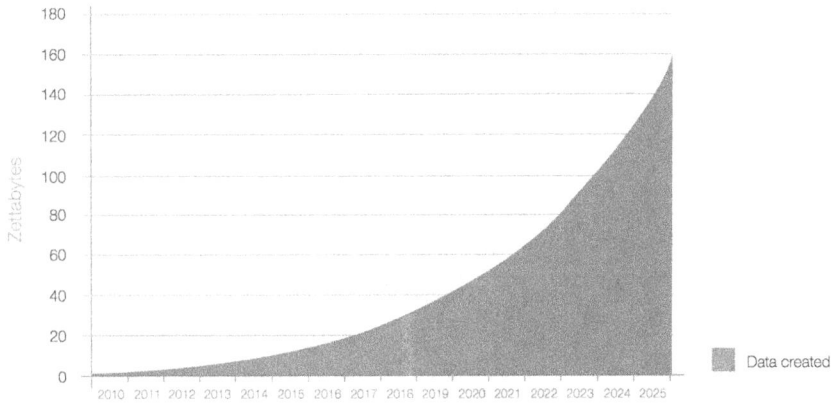

Explosive growth of digital data stored since 2010. Forecast as of September 2022
image by statista

Aligning with explosive growth of the use of the word liminal is the amount of digital data. This chart is a literal example of unknowability. For what even is a zettabyte, that is growing so rapidly? Well, it's 1,000,000,000,000,000,000,000 bytes. Yup, that's 21 zeros. Not sure that helps. Does it help to say that 160 zettabytes is like stacking 40 trillion DVD's to the moon and back 100 million times? Maybe. Some of us can picture what a DVD looks like. More than all the grains of the sand on earth? Even those that live in this data-centric world have a hard time making the magnitude of this understandable. For our purposes it is only necessary that we come to grips with this new resource, data. It has, is, and will continue to be a resource that changes our world. Fast.

While we are making obvious use of it everyday in our lives, not so obvious is how this resource is changing leadership, both the organization-building and execution functions.. You will hear of companies that are data-driven. Capital One was founded on "information-based strategy," a famous sign around Amazon headquarters is "In God we Trust, All Others Bring Data." There is a growing trend of organizations whose strategy falls under the guise of 'AI and analytics first'."[48] In the last 40 years entire new industries have emerged to mine and analyze the incredible flood of data that has come our way. Universities have added new colleges and curriculum to not only put a stronger emphasis on analytics, but combine it with culture-changing skills. They are creating courses such as Managing People and Teams and Organizational Leadership within their analytics schools.

The objective in all this is better decision-making. But take heart, data is a resource and analytics a tool, not the truth. Before we get too concerned, we humans with our experiences and inspiration have the ultimate value. Even Jeff Bezos reminds Amazon employees that many important decisions are made on "intuition, taste and heart,"[49] informed by data.

Organizations founded before the information revolution are in catch up mode. These cultures face huge changes. Much of the leadership literature and writing about data and analytics focuses on the leadership culture change necessary; for the technology exists. We are just still in the process of figuring out how to use it. Chief Information Officers are expected to become more holistically focused on how data and analytics inform their a company's strategy, and partner with the other functions. Other leaders are expected to integrate analytics more holistically into their operations. It's messy, just to be clear. These organizations don't have the magic bullet. A CEO survey found most of them were disappointed by the lack of returns their multi-million dollar investments in analytics and related data technologies were returning.[50] But they also knew that it would be a non-starter to go to their board or shareholders and say they were dis-investing in this capability. We are learning fast and furiously how to use this resource and create the culture changes in our organizations to do so.

As leaders in the Church, this is important to take seriously. The use of data and associated tools is becoming more and more the norm in every vocation, and the ability to make better decisions using this resource will continue to bear down on us. As we collaborate in organization-building leadership functions, more and more of the people in the room will work with this in their daily realities. It is part of the 21st Century culture. In 25 years, data-informed ministry decisions will be normal. We have an opportunity to steward this change and create the future so that it serves our Kingdom mission.

Mindset

But we have to decide to do so. For data does not insist on itself. It does not show up at the meeting uninvited. It does not raise its hand to speak. It does not ask for an appointment. It does not buy lunch. It does not have an agenda. If one of the foundational tenets of Godly discernment is indifference, we will find no perspective less indifferent than the behavior of people expressed through data. So data has to be invited. Questioned. It has to be valued, and it will respond. And because it has no agenda, it may not show you what you had hoped or what you thought you knew. Or it may. But it will almost always lead to insight and new questions.

Amber Smart is on the data forefront within the Church world. She and her team at SmartMetrix work with for profit, non-profit and Church leaders. She sees her for-profit clients respecting, having appreciation for and an appetite for data. They understand how it helps them accomplish their mission, whatever that mission may be. While she is happy for the for-profit work, her heart is for the local church and its leaders. Smart was deeply involved with the team that created the You-Version Bible app and then the multitude of data analytics and tools that continue to inform LifeChurch leadership in their innovative and generous far-flung ministry. She has witnessed the potential and knows the opportunity church leaders have to employ the resource of data for the good of all. In her vision, she sees the Church lead the way in stewarding this resource for God's glory. Her journey started there as a way to learn in uncharted territory. It is possible. But there are hurdles.

The first hurdle is us. Richard Rohr, when reflecting on serving two masters, reminds us "mammon" was the god of wealth, money, superficiality, and success. He shares the Jesuit heritage that defines 'mammon illness' as when we think all of life is counting, weighing, measuring, and deserving. Later in his reflection he paraphrases Luke in saying "You cannot move around inside the world of Infinite Grace and Mercy, and at the same time be counting and measuring with your overly defensive and finite little mind." He explains the difference as God's abundance world view versus our scarcity world-view. God is nothing but infinite, and we spend our time reducing Him by racking up and celebrating our multitude of failings.

So what do we do with this perspective? Is this all we need to dismiss any use of counts and numbers and measures in our leadership? Or is Rohr saying the way we use these things is the problem–our addiction to them as a replacement for God in our lives and our ministry? If we believe we are going to count and measure and judge ourselves and others in comparison to one another as the way to form our identity, our worth and our value then indeed, we must 100% agree "we have to stop weighing, measuring, and deserving in order to let the flow of forgiveness and love flow through us." Are we like the alcoholic, whose only option is to not drink at all, for even a sip will begin to move us away from freedom and life to the full? For as we have asserted, in and of themselves, numbers, counts, data and measures are indifferent, though like mammon our response to them is less so.

We have to wrestle with this as the wave of data and measures will be present in our meetings, in our minds and in our people. What does it mean to be culturally equipped to navigate this reality? We have figured out how to have money in our culture, in our churches, in our minds and in our people. We go to some extent to redeem this resource: we re-frame it for what it is and what Godly righteousness looks like when stewarded well. We use numerous Biblical illustrations for guidance. May not the same be the case here?

This question of whether measures, counts and data are to be avoided like alcohol to the alcoholic, or are redeemable through *spoude'* diligence-type organization-building leadership is one each of us has to answer in our own reflection. We and those close to us can best reveal our motivations and our addictions. Perhaps others are to steward this aspect of the ministry, or perhaps we are the ones that need to show a new path. We assert that measurement through use of counts and all forms of data are not something to be avoided, but something to be redeemed–by those of us who have been entrusted with leadership of the Church–and that if there is a problem to be addressed, it is with us. We measure. What we measure matters. And as those with organization-building responsibilities, we get to determine what that is.

Summary: The information revolution has changed the game. Much like the Gutenberg press in the 16th Century's Great Reformation, digital storage and our use of data is more quickly changing our 21st Century landscape. While we are not fully understanding what it is capable of bringing us in church leadership, we are responsible for stewarding this resource for the future Church, as we do our human and financial resources for our current form. We may well need to reframe the use of counts and measures in our church leadership mindset. It would be prudent to do that sooner than later, for it truly matters.

Chapter Twelve

Church and measures, so far

Given one of our organization-building leadership functions is to selectively forget the past, only bringing forward what will be useful in the future, let's take a look at the past as it relates to data and measurement.

Our 20th Century measures and subsequent data collection as local church leaders are pretty focused. We behaved as though we had agreed to "standards." At the base of all standards is the count of worship attendance at the weekend worship gathering(s). It is how we categorized local churches as well as membership within our denominational distinctions. Small, medium, large, mega and other size descriptors are used, though we all know that a medium sized United Methodist Church and a medium sized non-denominational church are not the same size. The other side of our standard coin is money. Given, spent or sent away. With worship attendance as the denominator, we could come up with ratios or giving per week per attendee or an alternative time period that allowed us some comparisons to see how we were doing. Research and consulting groups surveys offer benchmarks to give leaders a sense of what average, healthy or vital churches like themselves might expect. It helps us determine where to focus our leadership energy. Since these were the two church leadership cultural measures, they became the de-facto success criteria. We are familiar with some of these resultant "rules of thumb" ratios as a result.

Worship attendance growth as a percent versus same week a year ago; average giving per attendee; average new worship attendees per week, including second and third time attendees; first time givers, including repeat givers; new members per year; staff spending as a percent of overall spending and as a ratio to worship attendance; new Christians as percent of worship attendance, baptisms as a percent of worship attendance; as examples.

As we approached the 21st Century, worship attendance was declining culturally. Despite the herculean efforts of the last 40 years to stem this decline we have not altered this trajectory. A related decrease in people and priority for voluntarism of church work gave rise to the understanding that participation in small groups outside of the worship gathering, serving on teams, and serving in the community was important. So we have new ratios to guide us such as percent of attendance involved in small groups; ratio of small groups to worship attendance; serving volunteers as a ratio to worship attendance; as further examples.

As we closed out the 2010's, a sampling of the number of counts and measures of attendance at gatherings and groups, as well as money collected and spent reveals the extent of our focus. The United Methodists collect 130 unique data points for each of their 30,000 congregations, and determined some 25 measures to benchmark one another. The Episcopal church has 54 such counts. A survey of 12 of the largest non-denominational churches found 96 counts and measures.[51] These three examples are illustrative only. Though it is rare to find exceptions no matter the denominational or network affiliation.

In the 1990's we began to look not just internally, but externally to people around us. Quantitative demographic data was added to our portfolio of tools. Organizations such as MissionInsite and EASIdemographics brought new perspectives about those we didn't know as part of our congregations. Research organizations headed by The Barna Group brought us new perspectives on our congregates and people in culture from a qualitative standpoint. We could begin to compare our own congregations to the communities around us, demographically and behaviorally. We began to see the bigger picture. It was the bigger picture that alerted Mike Regele to write the *Death of the Church*. The data has been trying to tell us something.

So experiments began. We will share these examples to bring awareness of the movement that has started. While it is far from complete, these and other initiatives have changed the conversation in a way that is permanent. This is evidence that we are addressing our second leadership challenge of optimizing our present.

One project was the Reveal survey by Willow Creek Church in Chicago. We discovered many of our assumptions about how the activities and ideas, in which they famously and diligently invested, were not translating into the changes they prayed for and desired. The Reveal survey showed involvement in church activities does not predict or drive long-term spiritual growth. Due to Willow Creek's influence, thousands of churches took this survey, revealing a systemic issue, not just a one local church-specific issue. A series of Reveal books, starting in 2007 and updated as recently as 2018 document the learnings. While there are points of disagreement on methods, and interpretations, it cannot be denied this opened up a fresh way to think about measures. The leaders were open to a massive assumption being challenged. They collected new types of data for insight. This is a great example of a *spoude'* type organization-building leadership function; and it changed the conversation.

A second initiative was the United Methodist Church introducing dashboards in the United States at the Conference and local church levels. These dashboards were aligned with what focused research and analysis showed were the five drivers of local church vitality. Will Willimon, the North Alabama Bishop at the time and early adopter of the practice, summed up the reasons in 2011. "Our Conference has pioneered the use of metrics in our ministry in our Conference Dashboard. Our Dashboard shows the spiritual health of the churches each week showing the most reliable indicators of spiritual vitality, not only of a church's participation in Connectional giving, but also of professions of faith, baptism, attendance and service to those in need. Others in the United Methodist Church are taking note and starting to follow our lead."[52] In reporting on this movement, The United Methodist Reporter framed up the debate: "Detractors say that dashboards are a mistake - a worldly tool that will turn pastors' focus from ministry to 'making the numbers.' But advocates assert that dashboards offer a desperately-needed tool, in the face of steep declines in the denomination's membership, to create accountability for pastors, mobilize laity and boost congregational vitality."[52] In his 2012 book, *Bishop,* Willimon goes much deeper into his perspective on the value of measurement: "Immeasurement robs pastors of the joy of saying, "God did this through me," or, "I am going to improve in this area and measurement will confirm when I improve." [54]

As a result the national General Conference of the UMC instituted a Vital Signs initiative and it changed the conversation. An excellent primer on the value of this project is outlined in Gil Rendle's 2014 *Doing the Math of Mission, Fruits, Faithfulness and Metrics.* To say this initiative has been widely praised would be wrong; the varying perspectives still exist. It is a huge change in leadership culture and, therefore, has been a petri dish for learning how systems change, or not. It has been influential nonetheless.

Third is the work of Leadership Network from 2017 to 2021 with well resourced churches looking at the engagement process, the journey of people within a local church. Our largest churches mined the data resources they had collected over the years, and using the new resource of big data to enhance what they already had, began to ask new questions. For example, what actually occurs with people individually and collectively as they engage the invitations, programs and people of the church? How long does it take for a person to become fully engaged? Does it differ based on age and/or life stage? Over four years, four cohorts explored this in a project that was dubbed "Engagement Accelerators." We are familiar with most of the 35 participating churches, including North Point Church in Atlanta, Crossroads Church in Cincinnati, Lake Pointe Church in Dallas and Southeast Christian in Louisville. While it is hard for many local church leaders to relate to these churches due to their size, scale and focus, they provide a unique Kingdom benefit for their ability to explore new territory and take bigger risks as a result. They are incredibly focused on their visions and missions, and willing to change what is necessary to fulfill them.

They measured the entire process around people's response to executional leadership efforts to attract, keep, grow and multiply disciples. This is yet another marker of the emerging movement of using data as a resource find useful measures in support of leadership decisions. Another book resulted from this initiative, 2021's *Fourteen Fridays, A story of baseball, church, data, and redemption* by Eric Swanson and Matt Engel, the conveners of the accelerators. This book offers some very practical real-world insights into the possibilities of using data and measures in experimentation and learning within a church context. It highlights the key learnings from the accelerators, and how any of us can begin to apply them today.

Summary - It is well known we used the measures of counting attendance and money as the standards for measurement of ministry decisions. It is well entrenched in our mindsets. However, we have become increasingly convinced there have to be better measures and better approaches to discovering them; and have begun to experiment with the new questions, new data, and new tools.

Chapter Thirteen

Church Measurement Tools

Tools we do have

As a result of the explosion of digital data collection and the search for helpful insights there has been a dramatic increase in the tools that create, analyze and promise to solve problems for us. And they do, to the extent they can. These tools advance us beyond writing data on paper and storing the pages in a file; occasionally summing all the individual papers onto a new sheet. Or entering the data in Excel spreadsheets and using the automated functions to create new reports and charts and graphs. These methods are comfortable, but are time consuming, error-prone and not easily updated. We have been able to automate the flow of data and its reporting, which has made it possible for us to process more data than ever before. There are a number of examples of what has occurred over the past decade.

In the financial giving arena (where we have lots of good historic and current data) Mortarstone (2012) and Kingdom Analytics (2017) use individual level giving data to provide insights for those working in the area of financial steward-ship. Based on the learning, they append other data about the congregation and those around it for additional insights and potential ways to engage. Online giving tools and apps have grown dramatically and add to the data resources available for insight analysis.

Numerous digital communication and app development firms provide dashboards, data and analytics for online en-gagement with websites, social media platforms, email and online advertising. Church branded apps are used to connect people, while sharing resources that also collect data on our behaviors. Private or church-focused social networks such as Commissioned or Involved are emerging to give alternatives to Facebook. We collect data about our facilities usage and event participation through the geo-fencing of our campuses.

Church management systems (ChMS) are adding more ana-lytics capabilities to better use the data that they store. These systems are designed to automate many tasks that otherwise would be burdensome and time-consuming, and as a result, have collected a treasure trove of data as a resource. It is important to understand these systems are not designed as a tool to support measurement, so there are challenges. But some are slowly addressing that. ACS has extended its ability to bring more data to the table through acquiring Mission Insite (a leading church demographics firm). ROCK RMS (re-lationship management system) is designed to make it easy to collect the data you desire and automatically share it with powerful analysis and visualization tools that specialize in this work (tools like Tableau, Domo, and Power BI). Rock RMS can also host the website to facilitate data collection and merge it with ChMS data for additional insights in behaviors. A recently announced partnership between Rock RMS and Life Church is intriguing. PushPay is an example of ChMS that has continued to acquire and integrate various automation tools into one application, which is helpful in organizing the various pieces of data collected into one place. Of course, this list is nowhere near exhaustive in this market of over 150 ChMS options.

Life Church provides tools for free that have a data collection and analytics built in. Church Metrics for attendance and resource collection is easy to use immediately. Church OnLine hosting platform allows you to see data from online viewers. YouVersion Bible app is enhancing its analytics and visualization capabilities to learn more about who is using it and how it is being used.

A most wide-ranging investment in providing a data platform and tools of all sorts is from gloo of Boulder, Colorado. Founded in 2013, it is a technology platform dedicated to connecting the faith ecosystem and releasing its collective might. They have a number of partners, including Barna Research, which provides insights through research and tools like The State of Your Church assessment. In partnership with Harvard Flourishing project there is visibility into 6 flourishing personas to see what outcomes people are experiencing in their lives. gloo are the stewards of The Reveal survey, and they currently provide the data and analytics backbone to connect those that respond to the Jesus Get Us campaign to local churches, and with Generis to provide generosity insights. A partnership with Church Fuel gives access to the on-line course Data Fueled Church to assist in implementing the insights documented in *Fourteen Fridays*. They recently announced the "AI & the Church Initiative" to empower the Church to navigate this unknown landscape of artificial intelligence.

The development and use of these tools is a varied and ever-changing, still in its infancy. It is inspiring to see there are people called to this work and sacrificially investing millions of dollars in tools and resources to support church leaders in their mission. This is evidence of a movement; of the technical innovation that is occurring.

However, these tools are useful primarily in supporting executional leadership functions, the *ergasia* of diligence; and that makes sense. That was what they were designed for, because that is where our leadership energy has been focused. On executing church work.

Tools we don't have

Current tools are not designed to support the needs of the organization-building Leadership functions, the *spoude'* of diligence. And why would they be? We are just coming to terms with the need for the need to reclaim these leaderships functions. So what's the difference?

The book *Fourteen Fridays* has Colorado Rockies baseball games interwoven throughout the story. So, let's extend the theme. Say our churches worship gatherings 'lead the league' in attendees/month. Our youth ministry won the Cy Young award as the best 'discipler' for its growth. And our small groups ministry got the Most Improved award last year as many new groups started. We reward the people involved in leading these areas and urge them to continue doing what they are doing! They executed brilliantly.

However, our team record was 63 – 99, last in the division and out of the playoffs for the 8th straight year. As a result, we have infighting among members of the staff, camps have developed around the ministries that were doing well. We, those with organization-building leadership roles, the general manager and the manager get fired. Again. Now we know baseball is a finite game, and what we lead is an infinite game, but the principles are true. If the church community is not moving in the direction that Christ is leading, the people feel it, the community loses and we, as those responsible for the organization-building leadership, are ultimately accountable.

Organization-building leadership has concerns about different things beyond execution leadership. We are concerned that all the parts and pieces of the church are working together well, the executional leadership functions are strong, that the stewardship of the resources of people and money are creating the impact they desire. We are the ones responsible for ensuring "the whole body, joined and held together by every supporting ligament, grows and builds itself up in love, as each part does it's work."

As we grope for answers in our current liminal space church leaders approach Amber Smart to see if data can help them solve the two problems that keep them awake at night: worship attendance is not-rebounding post COVID, and giving that was initially strong, now is also waning. The power of our old standards is still strong! But now we are asking new questions, like what can the data tell us? What should we be doing differently? What is working and what isn't? So as we look at the data and how it is collected, the first challenge becomes obvious: we have systems, tools and resultant data pools that supported the executional ministry of the past, but don't answer the new questions being asked. Far from it.

The way through this challenge is not to handicap the executional function by asking us to use new tools when working tools already exist. We have to continue to optimize the present, and these tools help with that! The way through is, instead, for organizational leaders to define the overarching measures, and work backwards to create the tools that organization-building leadership function needs to build upon these executional systems.

But before we build the tools, it is best to really understand what the job is we are trying to accomplish. Only then can we assess our current suite of tools to see if what we need already exists, or if there is an existing tool that can be tweaked to accomplish the task. If not, we will need to create what is required. In any case, it is a technical innovation opportunity. Easily accomplishable if we have the will.

Summary: as leaders, we have data collection and analysis tools that have served to give us insight on church gathering attendance and the stewarding of money. While these tools help us make better decisions in these two areas, we are aware this does not mean the church, or related organization such as a Transformative City Network, is progressing towards its mission. We need tools to assist the leaders responsible for organization-building to learn more holistic perspectives and how well the organization functions, as well as understand the resulting effects this has on its stakeholders and society. The technology is available. With collective effort, we can enable it for Kingdom good.

Chapter Fourteen

The New Measures

Some of us have turned to this chapter immediately. Let's just cut to the chase. What are the new measures? You'll be disappointed if you expect the one for one replacement for in person worship attendance. You will be excited if you know in your heart of hearts that the answer is a more nuanced than that. For we have just moved into the organization-building leadership role of creating the future, together.

When COVID hit us hard in March of 2020 we could no longer gather, and one of our standard measures went to zero. We felt the implications immediately. As we adapted to on-line worship gatherings we groped for new ways to count and measure the old standard. We had hoped a quick and easy best practice answer would come from LifeChurch, as they had been working deeply with online church for some time. In April of 2020 Pastor Greg Groeschel addressed the question that seemed to be on everyone's minds at the time: What should we be measuring online when it comes to video? He opened by saying "I am really going to tell you my firm belief, and it may be a little frustrating to you.... you cannot compare with any other church." He went on to explain that LifeChurch has specific approaches and things they do, and the measures they use and the expected levels of success are meaningful to them alone. For they know the why behind the what. To compare or adopt their approach would not be helpful, since it is unlikely any other organization is exactly like Life Church. "You want to find different metrics to measure your success.... Determine what is success for you. Measure that week after week". He went on, "I don't know what matters to your church. I do know some things that matter. If you define clearly what matters, then you measure it best you can."[55] He articulated the Strategic Pathing step one and two from chapter ten.

For only those of us with organization-building leadership responsibility in our unique contexts and mission will be able to discover the new measures. While we may desire that one or two new measures be decreed by others, let's not get our hopes up. We have work to do. And the sooner we accept that the better. Perhaps in a few years our collective work will, indeed, unearth some universal insights. Let's view that as an unintended outcome, serendipity, not the goal. Our goal must be to one day see what we cannot yet see, to learn what we do not know.

At the 2022 Radiant Network conference a panel discussion alluded to the journey ahead, "We need measures to make the transition...to see the movement...of long obedience in the same direction." [56]

Amber Smart calls it a mind shift from certainty to curiosity.

We've called it a shift from measures as judgment to measures as learning.

City Transformation Network leaders call it a shift from local church centric to Kingdom centric measures.

Leadership thinkers in other disciplines see us moving towards better questions, not more clever answers.

If we can shift our mind-sets in these ways, we will reclaim the power of the organization-building leadership function.

Seth Godin outlines this challenge well: "System innovations (our social and institutional innovation work) almost always involve rejecting the standard metrics as a first step in making a difference. When you measure the same metrics, you're likely to create the same outcomes. But if you can see past the metrics to the results, it's possible to change the status quo."

Over the last few years we've been working on this very process and there are some characteristics that are emerging from the early experimenters in defining the new measures. Here is what is emerging.

A Foundational Few

"...Choose metrics extremely parsimoniously – pick as few as possible and make sure these are 'the irreducible core' that are feasible to measure and maximally affect progress."[57] This quote came from doctors on the Committee on Core Metrics for Better Health at Lower Cost at the Institute of Medicine. This is a field in which experience and opinions alone are insufficient as physical health, well-being and early mortality are on the line.

Parsimoniously is a tough word. It's worth looking up because the synonyms can make us cringe. But the point is clear: as few as possible. And that has many advantages.

The discipline and rigor of eliminating potential measures raises the energy on finding the best. This is exactly the *spoude'* diligence we are called to. It forces us to critique our assumptions, gut feelings, strongly held opinions and convictions. It forces us to collect data that will inspire us to actually change. This leads to conversations taking place between leaders for the first time about how change really happens. This creates new ways of thinking, new paradigms. It leads to unity of purpose, approach and hope.

Parsimoniously choosing is also vitally important so as to be actionable throughout our organizations. With this clarity we each can find our role in the measurement process, and we begin to see our interconnectedness.

Finally, it reminds us what is important. Clarity is kindness. Clarity is short. It ends with a period. It is not this, and this, and this, and this ending with an etc. and dot, dot, dot. It's this. It leads people away from the status quo, slowly but relentlessly.

Our Foundation is Relational

In work that has been done to this point with local churches and transformational city networks, as we narrow it down to the 'core', there is one consistent theme. The strength of the network of relationships within a church and outside of the church is the ultimate difference maker. It is what catalyzes change. We've sort of always known that, but have not taken the steps necessary to fully understand what this means. And while relationships are not as easily measured through counting, they can be mapped. We will explore this new measurement system later.

Relational is Collaborative

We know our missions and context put us in connection with other people and organizations. We can do nothing with significant impact alone. The key to increasing collaboration intentionally is asking better questions, not having better answers. Through better questions, organization-building leaders can begin to experience the benefits of contrarian viewpoints within a shared leadership structure. Better questions open up the conversation with sectors of the city and other churches in the center of the Transformative City Network Venn diagram from chapter eight. And when we map the resulting relationships and their development we find patterns. Patterns that inform and give life.

Collaboration drives Impact

Impact is what we envision we are having. But what is it? One of the hardest functions of organization-building leadership is to name and describe what will be different because we exist. In very specific and constrained terms, not general ones. Many of the impact reports we produce are falling on deaf ears. They are activity and resource allocation reports that declare victory while the world continues to suffer. We can do better. And we are not pursuing this alone. Over the past ten years eleven dashboards aggregating and analyzing data from many diverse sources for advancing Health and Equity in the United States have been created.[58] This was done to ensure the systems that are working to solve these nasty problems can have a shared measure of their collaborative effect. They can help us see what we cannot see today.

Impact takes time

In our discussions, it is clear the type of impact we hope to make will take time. This is a result of our current liminal space reality. For such a time as this. Sasha Dichter, President of 60 Decibels, a company birthed out of Acumen focusing on measuring social and environmental impact is at the forefront of 21st Century measurement. He provides a helpful perspective. "So much of the important work we do with people involves a bit of effort and attention up front and then letting the things we've set in motion - ideas, suggestions, words of support, challenges - evolve over time. Our job is to remain present and available, but we don't have to do all the work. Two mistakes are possible. Putting off the first foundational conversation (the clock does not start) and thinking that the entire problem needs to be solved today, by us, right now. We can't force it, ideas need to take on a life of their own. People need time to work through their reactions, emotions and fears. Important things take time to process. Plans have interdependencies and interconnections. Great outcomes happen when we set things in motion early, remain available and present when needed, and let things run their course (with a few adjustments, based on our care and experience, by us when needed). Nature, and time are on our side.'"[59]

The tools and technology are available to do whatever it is we imagine, but we must first create the demand. As those with organization-building leadership roles, we can do this. Together.

Summary: Part of the leadership pilgrimage we must take involves the very hard, soul searching work of defining what it is we are to change for the better, how we will do it in our current context, and how we will know if we are contributing positively? Could anything be worse than to discover one day that our best efforts actually made things worse? Through asking better questions, we are discovering the pathway to identifying these measures. While there is not one shared measure, there are some shared principles we can apply.

Section IV - Embracing Visualization. What is required to make sense of and communicate what we are learning?

Above all, trust in the slow work of God.
We are quite naturally impatient in everything
to reach the end without delay.
We should like to skip the intermediate stages.
We are impatient of being on the way to something unknown,
something new.
And yet it is the law of all progress
that it is made by passing through
some stages of instability – and that it may take a very long time.

Pierre Teilhard de Chardin, SJ

> "I will give you the keys of the kingdom of heaven; whatever you bind on earth will be bound in heaven, and whatever you loose on earth will be loosed in heaven."
>
> Jesus. Matthew 16:19

Overview

Our new measures and mind-sets will require us to embrace the visual languages and power of data visualization to make the invisible work of the Spirit more visible. This discipline has been in development for some time, and has become an integral part of the information revolution. While still in it's infancy it offers us an alternative communication vehicle. It's dynamic nature allows us bring alive both change over time and relational network mapping. Adding elegant artistic design enables data visualization to be a powerful tool of influence. This tool in our leadership quiver enables sense-making of the movement of God by communicating in a way that transcends the limitations of words and numbers.

(Note. You will see some example in this section. They are illustrative only as they try to capture what is possible. However, there is no way to communicate the power and possibility of a visual language in a black and white static book page. The invitation in chapter twenty will allow us to access more of the digital possibilities)

Act V

You'll remember the cliff hanger from the end of Act IV.

Surely someone had figured out these tools for Church leaders. Right, right?

Wrong.

I searched high and low for anything and everything that could help. Nada. That drawing and those questions became a turning point in my calling.

One aspect was the visualization itself. I began researching and looking for the tools to make the drawing a reality for our local church. What was most compelling was the visualizations and the technology was starting to be developed for many disciplines. What was surprising was how little work there was being done in the area of information and visualization for church leaders.

Related to the compelling, the work of Manuel Lima[60] resonated deeply.

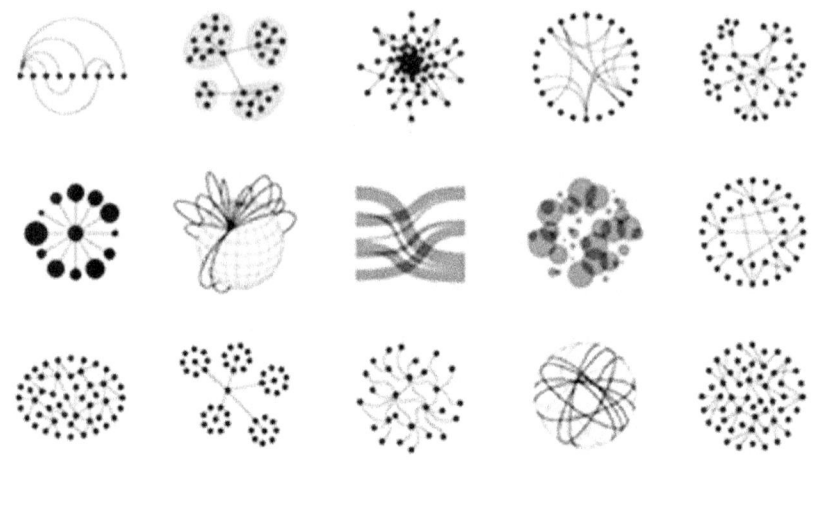

The Syntax of a New Language

From Visual Complexity: Mapping Patterns of Information.
image from Manual Lima

The concept of exploring a visual language was very exciting. What a great way to have new conversations. Not without its challenges of course, but it felt like a promising pathway. Looking back at my writing at that time unearths this gem:

If we can be open to learning, the movement of Spirit, we will also begin to ask fresh questions about how to be the Church, and as a result, lead the people with a vision that inspires growth. We will start to collect new data, and with that even more profoundly see the movement of God within our midst and in the world.

A perfectly reasonable response at this point would be to say, "well this is all very interesting, but unworkable" and go back to doing whatever it was we had been doing. For as previously mentioned, until this point my focus had always been 100% on whatever responsibilities I had at the local church.

But this idea caught my imagination and quickly became a passion. Part of the passion was that this idea works across many local churches, not just the one in which I held responsibility. Once our people venture out, they are immediately connected to others outside of our churches. This was bigger than our local church.

The other leaders of the church sensed my change in focus and were very supportive of me exploring this potential change in call. So, I started talking to people, telling my story and asking them what they saw God was doing to reform the Church. Then I asked them to recommend others who I should talk to, and said yes to just about anything I was invited to.

This brought me onto a number of projects with other local churches and regional denominational entities. At least three unexpected outcomes resulted from these efforts.

One. I ended up with two partners and we started our own business to pursue creating the tools we felt were missing for church leaders. Goodbye security and hello entrepreneurship. We set out with the mission to bring a new language of measurement, movement, connections, relationships, and impact. Started in 2014, it is far from being realized. But we began with what we felt compelled to do.

Two. The reason behind this became crystal clear: the love for the local church as a concept, turned into a more personal love and compassion for local church leaders. Pastors in particular. Pastors with names and stories. So while the journey of a non-clergy lay leader and subsequent staff member was clear to me, I learned more about the lives of ordained clergy in the local church than I had ever known before. I have to say, I had no idea.

The third outcome deserves its own act in the story.

Chapter Fifteen

Making the invisible, visible

The emerging science and art of data visualization provides great promise and hope for the organization-building leadership function for the future. We are staring into the abyss of the unknown and unknowable, societally and in our church expressions. And we see here with veiled faces. Scripturally we are told that "Faith is being sure of what we hope for and certain of what we do not see." So without a doubt we are the blind leading the blind.

While our faith gives us confidence to move forward, we need to report what it is we are learning and finding. Data visualization as a tool is mandatory in order to make any headway against the status quo. Good visualizations can show us when we are asking the wrong questions or need different data to discern new measures. This information is imperative for our pilgrimage.

According to the Interaction Design Foundation, data visualization is the graphical display of abstract information that assists us in two ways: sense-making and communication.[61]

To understand these two functions, let's look at Florence Nightingale. She pioneered a method for bringing about social change in the late 1850's. Though widely admired for her work in the military hospitals, bringing them up to civilian standards, she was obsessed with a sense of failure. 73% of men still died in the hospitals in Crimea. She knew without serious changes in the military, this would recur, and was unacceptable.

Sense-making.

Through the collection of vast amounts of statistics and by organizing them with tables and bar charts, Nightingale discovered that even in peacetime, soldiers died two times more frequently than civilians. The problem was more systemic than initially thought. Also, many of the assumptions about what happened in war-time hospitals were challenged. All of the leaders responsible on the ground were sure inadequate food and supplies lead to the deaths. The data and analysis proved it was a lack of sanitation. They had been solving the wrong problem for years. "We do not want impressions," she said, "We want facts." Ignoring advice from her mentor, she refused to present, in the normal manner, the facts to Queen Victoria to advocate for change. The best practice of the day was, according to her mentor, "The dryer (sic) the better. Statistics should be the dryest (sic) of all reading." Nightingale, though, was fearful of Queen Victoria's eyes 'glazing over."[62]

Communication

Bar charts, then 30 or so years old, were the current standard for visualizing data and were helpful to Nightingale in exploring the data and finding insight. While they would have been better than tables of numbers in presenting her findings, they lacked heart. So she designed the 'coxcomb' visual to "effect thro (sic) the eyes what we fail to convey to the public through their word-proof ears."[63]

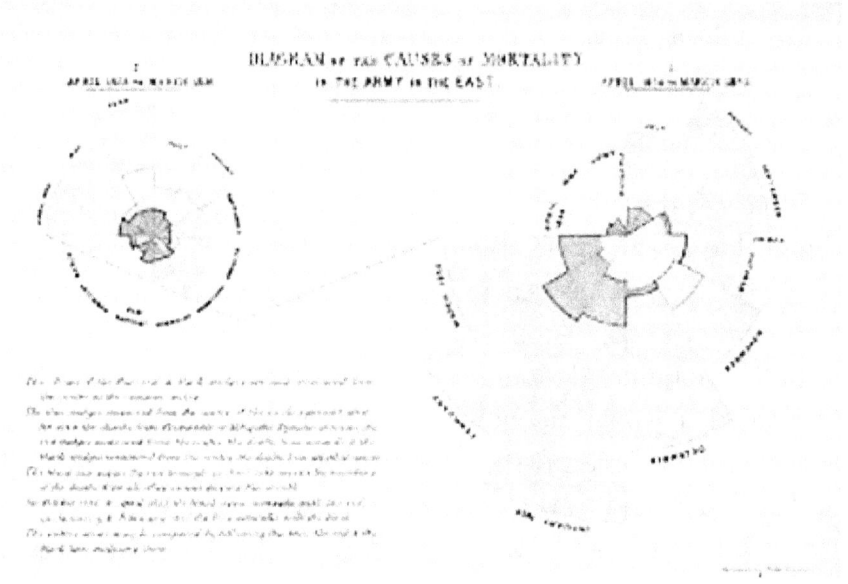

Diagram of the Causes of Mortality in the Army in the East. One of many novel graphics created by Nightingale.
Public Domain

Nightingale showed compassion through art in the data visualization. There is an elegance in her work. A compassion for the user, as well as for those she hoped to serve through its use. The raw science of it, which can drive new insights, can leave us cold. The tension Nightingale articulated is real for us because we too are in the people changing business. She was diligent in her leadership to ensure the people in her care received what they deserved. Her visual and subsequent work at the behest of Queen Victoria led to work that had an enormous impact. It resulted in systemic changes in the design and practices of military hospitals. By the end of the century, Army mortality rates were lower than those of civilians.

What if the insights and perspectives God would have us see are hidden by the face of business, or well-intended but poorly executed PowerPoint presentations and Excel spreadsheets? Art has been a powerful language for centuries for the Church, and it is a powerful culture creator. "It should do what only great art can do - elevate the spirit, help understand ourselves and the life around us, and give people the feeling they are not alone,"[64] Seel reminds us in *Network Power.*

Art tells stories that resonate with the head and the heart, and has done so for Christianity for 2000 years. It is time to reclaim the power of artistic tradition in our 21st Century digital space. The Church is called to lead in this way; to transcend either/or certainty and logic; and to make what is emerging visible. And we have the technology to do so.

Data visualization primer

This elegance of visualization does not come easily. Our 21st Century technological advances have democratized data visualization. Any of us can do it, and we do. We can click on a button in Excel or Google Data Studio and get hundreds of options to visualize any data set. We can do the same in PowerPoint to spiffy-up a presentation. We can use a free Infographic generator to make numbers look more human. Too often, our key success requirement for our resulting visualization is that it "Look cool" with some vague "I'll know when I see it" standard, or strangled to fit within our brand standard.

Elegant data visualization is a more thoughtful and professional approach. It uses the power of visualization to clarify exactly what the data says, through practices that protect the visualizer from intentionally or unintentionally confusing sense-making and communication. It comes from the user's perspective, not the creator's.

Together we are still learning what is possible. This is a relatively new field as the data, technical power and tools are a 21st century phenomena. But long held ideas and ideals have fueled this movement. An overview is provided on the following page. Highlighting some milestones in visualization are the late 1960's and early 1970's when Jacque Bertin published his theory of visualization book and John Tukey pioneered the use of visualization by computers. It was in 1983 that Edward Tufte began publishing his works which have become the basis for professional visualization for most everyone in the field today. Tufte's course, from the man himself, is available for anyone to attend even today. Tufte was dubbed "*The DaVinci of Data*" by the New York Times.

The Europeans are ahead of the US in creating and using visual languages. Much of the best practices today stem from sources originating there. This must be a result of the sheer number of languages and dialects and cultures calcified over thousands of years. To have an effective European economy they needed to do it. Or their cereal boxes would be 3 metres tall and look like what the Tower of Babel sounded like. A great starting point and portal into this field is www.visualizingdata.com from England's Andy Kirk.

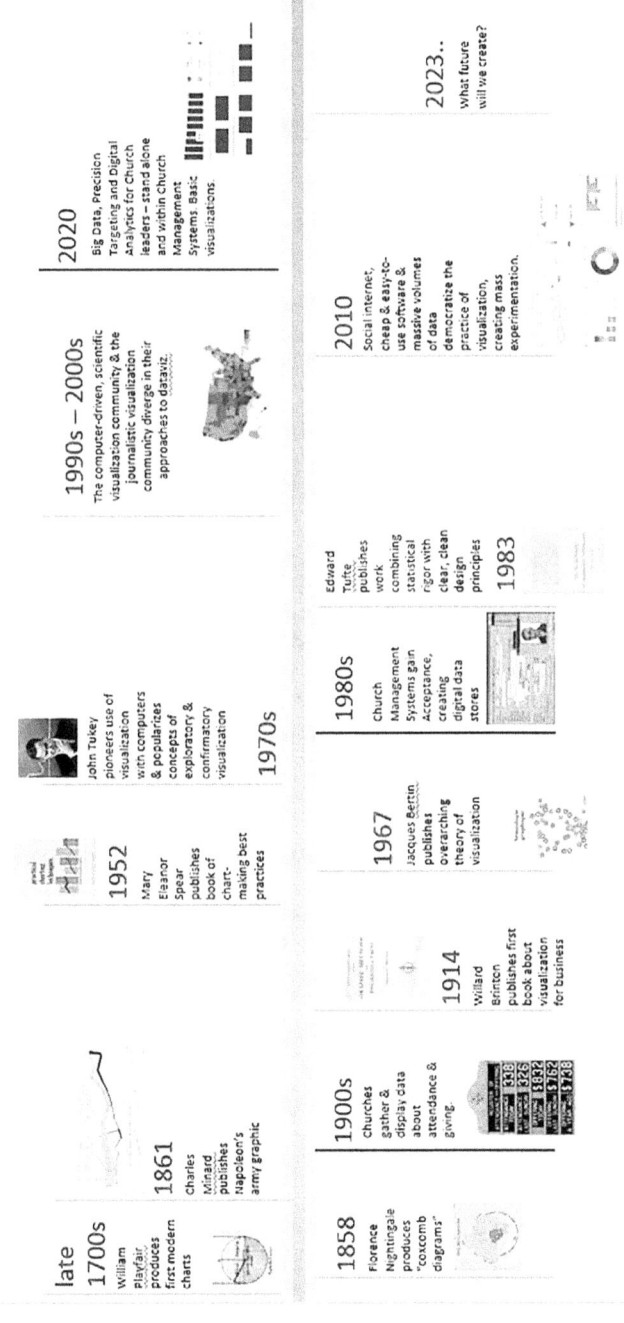

late 1700s
William Playfair produces first modern charts

1861
Charles Minard publishes Napoleon's army graphic

1952
Mary Eleanor Spear publishes book of chart-making best practices

1970s
John Tukey pioneers use of visualization with computers & popularizes concepts of exploratory & confirmatory visualization

1990s – 2000s
The computer-driven, scientific visualization community & the journalistic visualization community diverge in their approaches to dataviz.

2020
Big Data, Precision Targeting and Digital Analytics for Church leaders – stand alone and within Church Management Systems. Basic visualizations

1858
Florence Nightingale produces "coxcomb diagrams"

1900s
Churches gather & display data about attendance & giving.

1914
Willard Brinton publishes first book about visualization for business

1967
Jacques Bertin publishes overarching theory of visualization

1980s
Church Management Systems gain acceptance, creating digital data stores

1983
Edward Tufte publishes work combining statistical rigor with clear, clean design principles

2010
Social internet, cheap & easy-to-use software & massive volumes of data democratize the practice of visualization, creating mass experimentation.

2023...
what future will we create?

Data visualization is an even more immature field than data and measurement in its deployment. It does, however, offer us a new way of seeing and thinking. It is a "new wineskin" for our "new wine" organization-building leadership functions and responsibilities. And Jesus's teaching about new wine in old wineskins applies without reservation. If we try to make sense and communicate our senior leadership adaptations and new measures in the old wineskins, the status quo will prevail and we will be left with nothing.

As an example, let's look at a field where we do have data, but need to look at it with an organization-building leadership perspective. In this case, the collection and use of money. Normally, as leaders we would look at three different reports to understand our current state of financial health: revenue and expense statement, balance sheet, and cash flow statement.

A revenue and expense report makes it easy to see how much money is coming in and how much is going out. We normally break our expenses into varying types, depending on what the finance team prefers. Our balance sheets show us where are funds are, or claims we have against them. Our cash flow statements show us where cash was exchanged between the funds. These reports normally look like the dry table of statistics that Florence Nightingale eschewed. For example here a summary of some hypothetical selected data from these types of reports.

General Fund				Pre-School		
Revenue				Revenue		
Giving	Cash	200,000		Fees		200,000
Giving	Check	1,000,000		Grants		30,000
Giving	On-line	1,100,000				
Grants		125,000				
Fees		6,000				
Total Revenue		2,431,000		Total Revenue		230,000
Expenses				Expenses		
Program		882,000				230,000
Admin/Ops		940,000				
Global Missions		119,000				
Local Missions		223,000				
Total Expenses		2,164,000		Total Expenses		230,000
Net Cash		267,000		Net Cash		0

Designated Funds				Cash Position	
Revenue					
Giving	Cash	20,000		Operating	450,000
Giving	Check	190,000		Designated	400,000
Giving	On-line	205,000		Long-Term	150,000
Total Revenue		415,000		Total	1,000,000
Expenses					
Capital		375,000			
Net Cash		40,000			

These reports work fine if all we were doing was ensuring the accounting was sound and we are spending within budget. Accounting and finance people are whizzes at detailed financial reporting; but not everyone who is part of a leadership team speaks that language. As we recall, our communal leadership vision requires diversity in perspective.

And as organization-building leaders we also have the responsibility of ensuring our organization is funded for the long-term and the short-term, that the money we are spending is being spent where it needs to be in order to optimize the present and create the future, and that we can absorb any short term variances by having adequate cash available. The reader will remember chapter ten's strategic pathing document item #6, Resource Release. What if one visualization could show how well this is occurring?[65]

Giving →→→ Funds →→→ Expenses →→→ Cash

The Sankey diagram is a vastly underutilized data visualization. These diagrams show complex processes visually, and make sense of how information, dollars or people flow through a system. In this case, from sources of giving and revenue, to funds for various uses, to expenses within those uses, to cash available. Does interpreting a diagram like this require us to embrace a visual language, yes? But does a diagram like this also make it more likely for an entire leadership team to understand a topic, ask better questions, and begin to investigate varying observations, knowing that different people will see different things? Also yes. It is a great tool for learning and for insight.

This is our challenge and opportunity with data visualization, and it is good to know we have all we need. We just need to choose to be diligent in its development and application.

Summary - Data visualization is truly a tool for *spoude'* organization-building leadership, and is being developed to harness the power of the data explosion of the information reformation. As we are addressing more and more complex problems, the ability to see reality, make sense of it, and communicate what we are learning will be paramount. But we also need to apply *ergasia* diligence to its execution, due to its power. Beyond that, we have the opportunity to communicate artistically with our digital tools, inviting people into the visualization through beauty and elegance. No longer just cold graphs, but stories yearning to be told. We have much to learn in using it, and it will be worth the journey to do so.

Chapter Sixteen

Dynamism

Movement over Time

One of the capabilities our digital data visualization technology enables is to see movement over time. As organization-building leaders, a broader perspective of time is something we need to embrace. As an example, Edward Tufte names the 1869 visualization of Napoleon's March into and out of Russia in 1812 and 1813 a great data visualization.

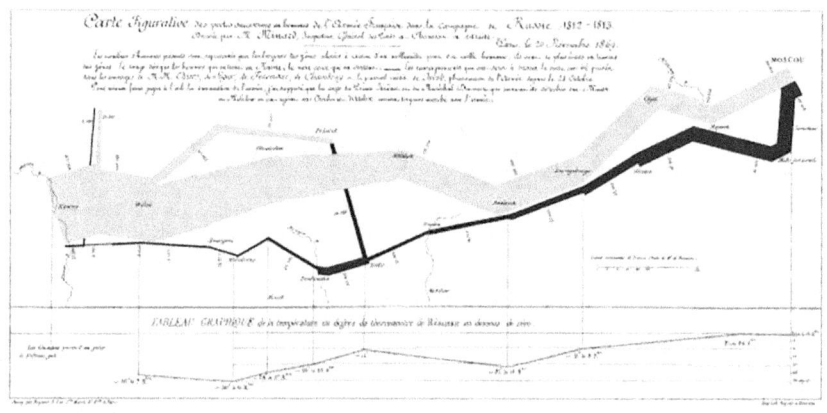

Napolean's March
Image by Charles Joseph Minard

What happened to his troops as they invaded from the left of the visual to the right, then retreated back to the left, tells the story.

This ability to tell a story as it unfolds over time is much greater today with digital and dynamic tools. But how do we think about time?

Earlier we reviewed the number of measures the Methodist, the Episcopal and non-denominational churches used. The vast majority of them are represented by changes we hope to see within the time frame of a week, or a few weeks at most, such as weekly giving or weekly attendance. Two notable exceptions are the measures shared by all which represent the second time frame we embrace–eternity. These are Baptisms and Professions of Faith.

These two time frames reflect the creeds of affirmation in which we bind ourselves. Even though our creeds affirm Christ's birth, death and resurrection, they traditionally skip over what happens in between. The life of Jesus Christ and His Way. However, our role as organization-building church leaders demands we live in the space between the week and eternity. This is the place where transformation happens in lives and communities, on the way to all things being made whole.

As we have confined ourselves to these ends of the time spectrum while sincerely desiring to do good works, we affix the promises of eternity to the behaviors of this week. We expect our work to change lives immediately, to fix problems quickly. When we sit down to craft our church's value statements, we refuse to use the word patience as a value. For when we think about that word on our website, or we tell our congregation the high value we put on patience for the outcomes and impact of our work to be seen and felt, we are uncomfortable. We don't believe our stakeholders would be supportive, so we tell them what they want to hear. We rationalize that is what other organizations promise, quick change, how can we do any less?

Would we not be better off to re-frame time, first within ourselves, and then with all stakeholders? Lift up the value of patience as the result of maturity in our faith? Connect with what the stakeholders know to be true and validate their instinct rather than enable their delusion? Is it not a Fruit of the Spirit? Beyond that, imagine if it could be seen that we can influence this time dimension? Can our impatience be the holy discontent that there are things that could be done, that we are just not doing? Can we show that if we are intentional in our leadership and our followership, then the things we desire can happen sooner than they would have otherwise? That our actions can loose the keys to the Kingdom and release the Spirit's power? It is frustrating that our progress to the things God's desire is slow, and patience is required to persevere. But as Seel outlines out in *Network Power*, a timely aspect we can employ is to start the change platform. "Once it is established, accelerating the growth and impact (through intention) can happen in an exponential fashion."[67] And that builds momentum.

If we choose to live and lead into this reality, we will need to help people make sense of this and communicate it well. The digital data visualization techniques that were used to tell the story of Napoleon's March are, today, much more multi-dimensional, dynamic and interactive. We have the tools to communicate the value of patience in the times between next week and eternity.

Imagine If

We remember that a key *spoude'* diligence organization-building leadership function is to embrace imagination. About what is possible. It has to come before we get to work in battling the status quo. Another movement that's been expressed over the previous twenty years is the imagining of networks as our Kingdom reality in envisioning the full expression of the 21st Century Church. And if we can imagine it, then we can implement it. Let's take a quick look at what has been imagined.

In 2021, David John Seel wrote the book *Network Power, The Science of Making a Difference.* This book is highly recommended as a primer on why the focus on networks is gaining strength for a time such as this. He writes "The substance of this book is not merely a pragmatic tool for organizational effectiveness, rather it is a reaffirmation of a *metaphysically relational reality.* Affirming the priority of the Trinity is reorienting our lives around what is most true about ourselves and the world. Dense networks are effective because they are true to reality. In traditional Christian terms, the Trinity is the *why* behind the *what* of dense networks. It is not just a good idea or a useful tool, it is the way reality works." When it comes to visualizing this reality, Seel contends "If we were graphing this visually, habitus are the lines connecting the various nodes. We see the nodes, but it is these invisible lines that put the nodes into a network. Though less obvious, they remain decisive."[68]

Mark Sayers notes in 2022's *A Non-Anxious Presence* the reality that "nature operates in a nonlinear fashion, more complex than complicated. We tend to treat problems as complicated, that can be solved in linear fashion." He shows a network diagram and asserts that we need to adapt to this reality.

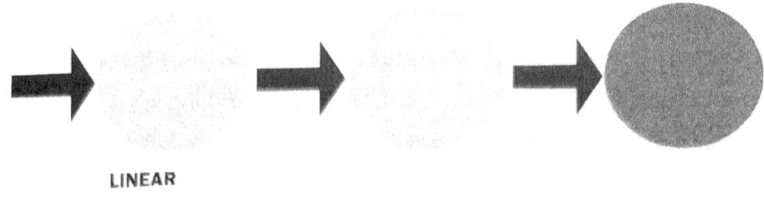

LINEAR

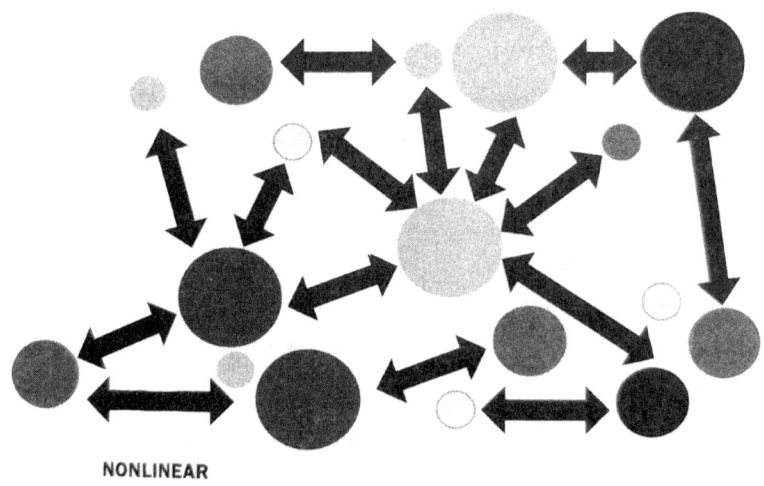

NONLINEAR

From Efficiency to Adaptation
image by Mark Sayers

A Field Guide to Methodist Fresh Expressions, published in 2020 by Michael Adam Beck and Jorge Acevedo, explores how the current form of church and a network of Fresh Expressions of church can co-exist in a blended ecology ecosystem, drawn as a relational network.

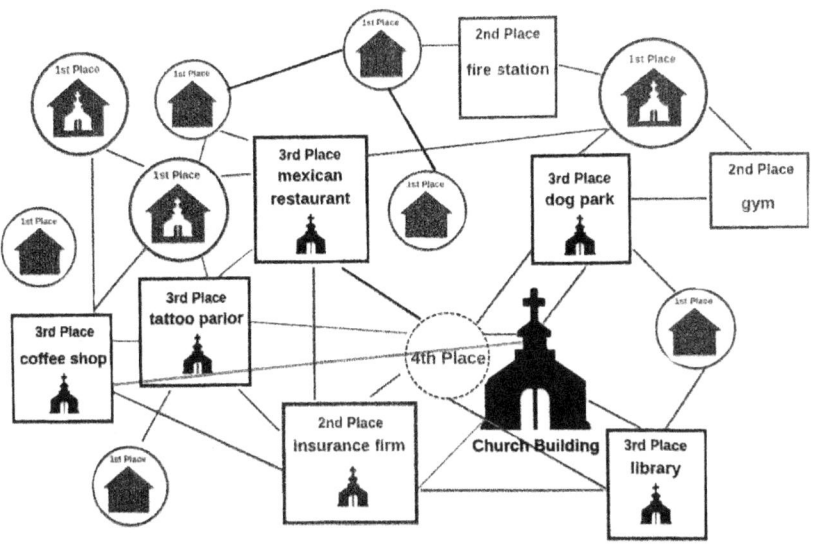

The Blended Ecology Ecosystem
Image by Michael Beck and Jorge Acevedo

In 2015, Alan Roxborough wrote *Structured for Mission, Renewing the Culture of the Church.* In this book, he challenges the church to use its imagination to see itself not as just an institution, but as an empowered people who can bring alive the essence of the church on a local level. He uses an electric power distribution network visualization to help us see what he means.

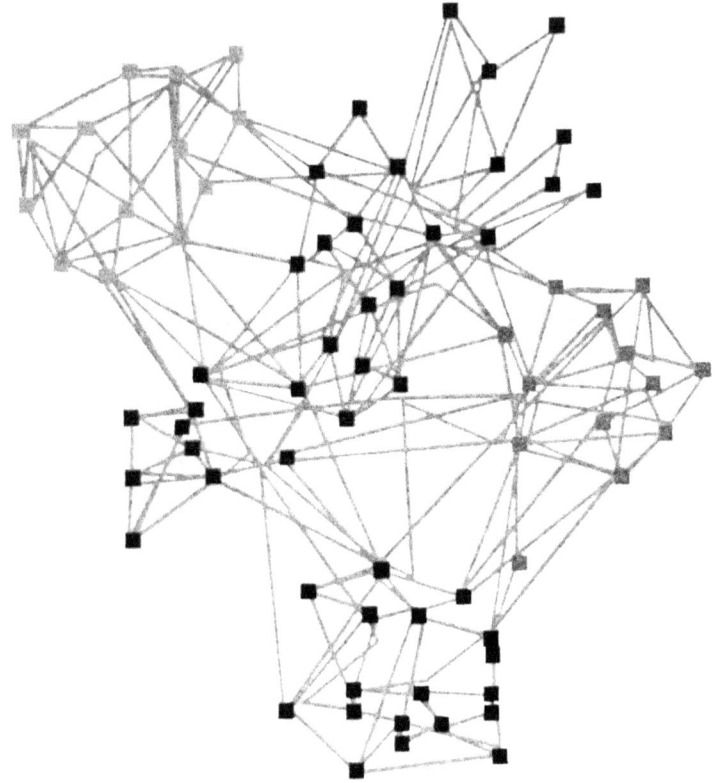

Distributive Systems
Image by Alan Roxburgh

In 2009 Dwight Friesen wrote *Thy Kingdom Connected, What the Church Can Learn from Facebook, the Internet and Other Networks.* In this work, Friesen makes the point that the Kingdom of God has always been a connected network and that the influence of social networks are a result of tapping into this truth.

Missional Linking

Missional Linking
Image by Dwight J Friesen

Also in 2009, Alan Hirsch in *The Forgotten Ways, Reactivating the Missional Church* reminds us that the network structure is the reason for the meteoric growth of the early Church, and asserts that the 21st Century is ripe for a recapturing of that essence for this power. This message builds off that of his 2003 book *The Shaping of Things to Come, Innovation and Mission for the 21st Century Church,* where the concept of networked people was introduced.

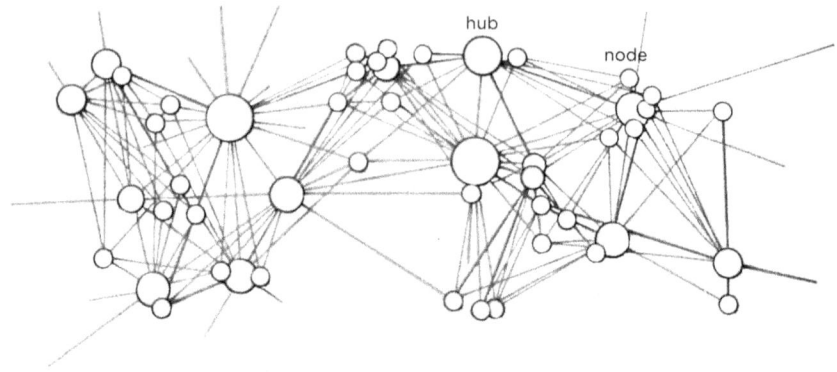

The Dynamic Structure of Networks
Image by Alan Hirsch

As we reviewed in chapter eight, during this same time period we have witnessed the rise of the Transformational City Network. These convening organizations connect not only church leaders to one another, but to people from all sectors of a city who desire their cities to be thriving and flourishing communities. One of the major proponents and catalysts for transformational city networks is Rob Kelly, the Founder and CEO of the For Charlotte Network, and cofounder (with Eric Swanson) of the City Leaders Collective, which connects, coaches and equips city network leaders for the flourishing of cities. Kelly, along with missiologist Alan Hirsch, directly address the power of network structures for accelerating missional efforts in 2023's *Metanoia: How God Radically Transforms People, Churches, and Organizations from the Inside Out.*

There are no doubt more references to this path forward into the unknown and unknowable for the Church. We can be excited by this as we all sense the same thing that Seel articulates: "Dense networks are the way to get things done in society. A mere collection of people or networks is not actually a dense network. The difference is the degree to which people have aligned themselves - ideally to their own motivations - to a shared cause. A dense network requires balancing a high degree of missional solidarity with relational sociability. A disparate collection of people must be consciously mobilized toward collective action. These are the weaknesses of most faith based organizations, who talk warmly of "community", but do little to mobilize its collective potential. There may be talk of individually reaching a particular city or neighborhood, but the emphasis continues to be on the individual action rather than the collective mobilization. Other organizations have a failure of imagination. They don't embrace with any confidence a big picture cause. Painting a particular school is hardly the same thing as reducing the illiteracy rates of elementary age students in a city. We tend not to think big enough."[69]

Every reformation that has occurred has happened this way, through the power of people networked with a shared common cause. Each chaotic inflection point of the Transitional waves was navigated in this manner. Even if it could not be seen or appreciated at the time, the whispers of people in relationship from village to village changed the world.

There is hope. There is a realistic adoptable path forward.

Summary: There are two aspects of the measurement of movement that data visualization that will help us make sense and communicate the reality of leadership pilgrimage. The first is the ability to see movement over time. To do so we will need to begin to operate in the months and years it takes for change to truly take hold. The second is the understanding of the power of networked relationships and how we might see and intentionally lead in a manner that releases that power for Kingdom purposes.

Chapter Seventeen

Network Visualization

We stated earlier that if we can imagine it, we can implement it. If we implement it, then we can see it. Maria Popova, of *The Marganalian* stated when commenting on seeing, "We change our seeing only when we change the way we look. When we change the tools for looking, or the instrument of the mind." Then when we see it, we can recognize it. When we recognize it, then we can change it.

The ability to bring to life what the authors have imagined regarding networks is with us today. We can change our tools, and the instrument that is our mind. The technological innovation of the network graph capability and field of understanding is in itself a related movement. It has been used in tracking complex financial dealings in fraud investigation, and in battling cell based terrorism warfare (in which relationships between people and entities are trying to be hidden). For the past twenty years Christine Capra and her growing network at sumApp have been developing this capability for use by the social services sector, particularly networks of people and organizations trying to address the systemic societal problems afflicting all of us. She and her team are living through the introduction of this visual language, and are the first to admit it is not instantly understood.

This is a picture of a social systems map of the Community of Practice who have joined Capra's network in various capacities, roles and commitments in the task she outlines below.

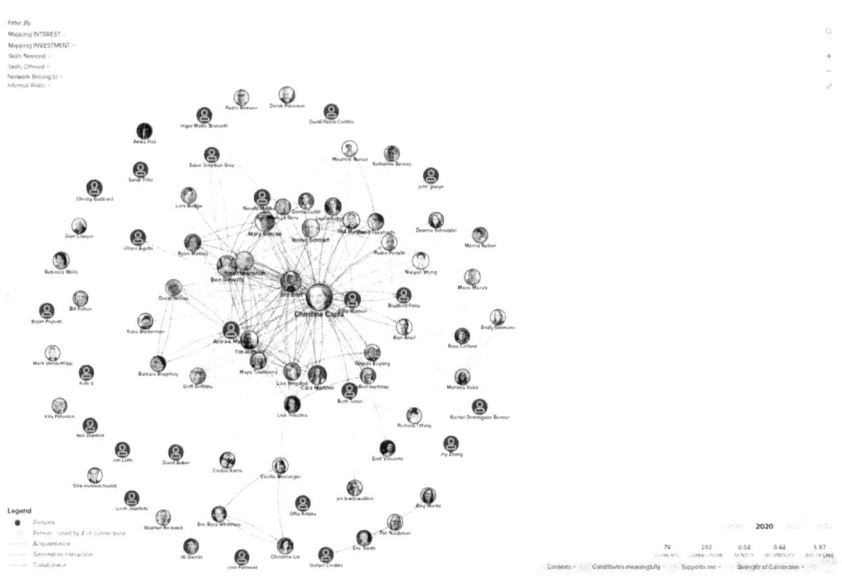

Social System Mapping Community of Practice
sumApp

Commenting on the network visualization, Capra says "And because it's new, because the media that use this language are not yet prevalent, because most people have had little exposure to it - to many people it's confusing and underwhelming. Beyond the fun of pretty moving pictures, and zooming in & out - it gets dull and irrelevant fast if you can't 'read' the language."[71]

But once we can read the language, whole new vistas are opened. We can compare this to the development of the geographic map, which is certainly part of the air we breathe today. We rely on maps in our daily lives, and can interpret them instantly. Beyond that, they are essential to society. And the practitioners in the field of cartography go so far as to say they shape society. But there was a day when the geographic map did not exist.

For us, the depth and texture of the Bible come alive with the maps of the geography of the Land of Twelve Tribes, Jesus's Ministry pilgrimage and Paul's Missionary Journeys. Reading the text and looking at the maps bring "Aha's" and insights to the reality of the story that the words alone cannot convey.

The network graph is not of geography, but of relationships. We can substitute the word relationship for geography in every sentence in the previous two paragraphs. We would even be proponents of saying relationships transcend geography when it comes to shaping society, understanding they are both powerful.

Capra continues and gives us a path forward. "Some of us are starting to be able to read the visual language of an interactive network graph the same way. Because of repeated exposure. Because we compose information using the language. Because we dig in and are curious and discover things.

My fantasy is that someday (sooner, rather than later, I hope) far more people will be able to read and write in this language. Because with all the wicked, seemingly intractable problems we currently face coping, adapting, solving them requires us to, collectively, have far greater insight and ability to communicate about connections - about the relationships within systems, between people, among organizations, etc. And the need for that insight and ability to communicate about those otherwise-invisible relationships is precisely what this new visual language emerged from. Its whole purpose is to increase our insight in ways nothing else can. I'd like us all to be increasingly able to take advantage of that purpose - the way we've latched onto geographical maps. In fact, I think it may be crucial to our survival."[72]

The nature of the network graph: it's dynamic, multi-dimensional, layered, ever-changing construction cannot be fully appreciated with a two-dimensional picture or detailed description. Especially when technology gives us a better option. There is a link in chapter twenty to experience, and if you so inclined, to experiment with it together. But fair warning, you will experience what this chapter promises. It proves what is possible. What happens with it is up to us.

The network visualization will prove to be the Holy Grail of visualizations that will serve the Church and related organizations into the 21st Century. It is the finest representation of power behind the priesthood of all believers and how the gospel will be spread, how disciples will be made, and how all people will experience the Shalom of God. It is the tool that helps us lead in the way of *spoude'* diligence, assisting us in adapting our leadership functions to what is necessary. It is a new wineskin for the new wine.

While we may not need any more information to start our leadership pilgrimage into the unknown, we do need a sense of safety. It would be easier, perhaps, if we did not have the option of an actual pathway. So much like the inchworm ensures a safe journey by staying connected to what is known as it explores new territory, the network map provides a tool to see the relational web of meaning and connectivity that will actually make the pilgrimage possible. It is this relational system God has woven into creation. In that, and our shared pilgrimage, we can take comfort as we venture into the unknown. And it is to this adventure we are called, the invitation is extended. We will next explore why redeeming measurement and embracing visualization will ease the resistance to change and enable our leadership adaptations.

Summary - Our journey into the unknown and unknowable will invite us to learn a visual language. Much like when geographic maps, once we become familiar with this language, we will find it indispensable. The network map technology will allow us to not only see our interdependence upon one another, but help us make the shift in our minds to understand and lead in the complexities of our time. And given that is our call with God, we can take heart.

Section V - Calling. For Such a Time as This. What does it mean to be called to leadership within the Church?

"This country... needs... no thin Idealist, no course Realist, but a man whose eye reads the heavens, while his feet step firmly on the ground, and his hands are strong and dexterous for the use of human implements... a man of universal sympathies, but self-possessed; a man who knows the region of emotion, though he is not its slave; a man to whom this world is no mere spectacle or fleeting shadow, but a great solemn game , to played with good heed, for its stakes are of eternal value, yet who, if his play be true, heeds not what he loses by the falsehoods of others; a man who hives from the past, yet knows that its honey can but moderately avail him; whose comprehensive eye scans the present, neither infatuated by its golden lures, not chilled by its many ventures; who possesses prescience, the gift which discerns tomorrow """ Margaret Fuller (May 23, 1810 - 1850)

"Lord Jesus Christ, Son of God, have mercy on us."   The Jesus prayer.

Overview

We have a calling as leaders within the Church. With that comes a responsibility to the One who calls us and to one another. The people of the 21st Century are yearning for the response through the Church. This response and responsibility are in perfect harmony. At the core of this harmony is the shift from independence to interdependence in our relationships at personal and organizational levels. To support this we need pathways and tools to help shift our minds from certainty to curiosity, from knowing to learning, from static linear change to dynamic complex change. There is a pathway forward.

We are undertaking a leadership pilgrimage rife with discovery and innovation, as we have described. It a journey for those who desire to contribute and participate in this co-creation of the future. We intend to provide a space to do just that; for such a time as this.

Act VI

We were way ahead of the market. Our commitment to creating the tools was strong. We built the data, analytics and visualization tools that we would have wanted as organization-building local church leaders. We started with the treasure trove of United Methodist data and research for our first iteration. The tool was ready for use and leveraged all the data that has been collected for years while seamlessly integrating demographic data and new data the tool itself collected.

It is called *vizchurch*. The home page of this analytic and visualization software reflects many of the tenets we thought were (and still know to be) important.

It is impossible to express the unqualified encouragement we received from Jeff Kimmel, an executive pastor who has been 'all-in' since day one. We so appreciated his willingness to be the guinea pig, offering to try anything to help accomplish his church's mission. He, Mike Harder [74], Tom Pasmore [75] and others provided the insight we needed, though did not necessarily want to hear.

What we learned was they did not know how to (or struggled to) gain acceptance beyond themselves to use *vizchurch* software in a leadership capacity. We even boiled the initial product down to a more bite sized morsel. Still nothing, despite excellent opportunities to showcase the work. We had built the product we had desired, but the leadership culture was not ready. It was an extremely tough time, costing considerable personal financial expense for our team and years of ours and others time. Not to mention, a part of our identities were wrapped up in this project. Alas, we proved again that we humans can apparently only learn by trying and failing. The hard way. It is safe to say this has not been the only time we bounced off the guardrails of the road we were invited to travel, though this one was the most likely to derail the pilgrimage.

A critical learning, that we see more clearly in hindsight, is this is the reality of the pilgrimage to pursue call and passion. Over time, painfully, we moved our focus from product development to market development. More specifically, the needs of leaders to navigate the future, and the role that data, measurement and visualization would play in that plan, if one existed at all.

We spent the next six years with the leaders, themselves. Listening, experimenting, developing, discarding, fending off the status quo, learning in different settings. Jeff Kimmel again has been instrumental in this. And once again, proving that God is in the redeeming business, the *vizchurch* work rekindled a 20 year old relationship with Eric Swanson, opening up entirely new vistas of insight, connections, conversations and collaboration.

It has also been a tremendous catalyst in our spiritual formation and discipleship. I resonate more deeply than ever with Gordon Crosby's assertion that growth "is based on a person being called to the inward life and the outward journey in the same group." These are not groups to strengthen each person in his or her individual mission, but in a corporate mission. So we've focused on this business of call, which is to say, 'This is God's call. I've got to do this.'

So be it. We press on.

"If you advance confidently in the direction of your dreams, and endeavor to live the life you have imagined, you will meet with a success unexpected in common hours. .... If you have built castles in the air, your work need not be lost; that is where they should be. Now, put the foundation under them." Henry David Thoreau

These last nine years have been a time of exploration and learning. While these chapters are short, the foundation under each is deep and has been crafted brick by brick. I did not know this as it was happening, I just wanted to be better at my craft. So I went about setting a foundation under this dream.

I realized I needed to learn some things about networks, so I did. The University of Pennsylvania offered a MOOC (love the term Massive Online Open Courses) on Social Network Science. A sociologist friend coached me up on the dynamics and realities on how groups and people interact. Meet Ups on Graph databases (best for network maps) and Programming became regular events. Professional classes with Neo4J, the graph database leader taught about the need for a new type of database to visualization and understanding of networked relationships.

Since I was moving into an self-employment role, it seemed that fund-raising to pay the bills would be important. I attended a week-long Lilly/IUPUI Philanthropy Religious Fundraising Workshop at St. Meinrad's monastery. I completed the Fundraising Essentials course at the Foundation Center in Washington DC. I worked at Starbucks for two years for health insurance and some bridge income. There I teamed with much younger people and witnessed the way things worked behind the scenes in a much studied organization. People from the church I served knew of the vision, and were generous in getting me started.

I knew data visualization was going to be important, but how would I learn that? My partners and I attended Tufte's course, which came with his five books on the subject. I have a signed edition of Cool Infographics from Randy Krum from his in-person workshop. I was mentored and coached by an employee of Keylines, a network graphing software leader. I am currently participating in SumApp's open collaboration community in the development of Social System Maps, learning through co-creating.

Discovering new ways to measure took me to two Acumen courses. Lean metrics by Sasha Dichta, who is now the president of 60 Decibels, is redefining what impact really is. Systems Practice helps ground us in the principles of what is necessary to cultivate a systems change. Engaging the work of Smart-Metrix to support our efforts has confirmed and expanded the thinking and what is possible in this area. My seven years as part of a CrossFit community has not only kept me physically fit for the task; but has demonstrated the efficacy of measurement paired with community in guiding and shaping behaviors in people.

Additionally, the CrossFit community of younger folks has brought the research of the generational world-view shift into flesh and blood interactions. Finally, it showed me how to do hard new things; the required path to growth and the journey ahead.

There has been ongoing learning with the larger Church. Participating as part of a team in the Leadership Networks Engagement Accelerator, and learning from the largest non-denominational churches as they advance the craft allowed us to share our work to help advance theirs. Assisting a denominational church in implementing their vision led to participation with Transformative City Network leaders in their work and workshops. I became active in regional and national denominational activities which brought new perspectives and connections. Here Phil McKinney's innovation work was introduced, along with other forward-thinking organizations perspectives.

What has become clear on this journey is that each of these areas of study and experience have contributed to the emerging picture. It is at the intersection of translating a dozen different disciplines through the lens of what it means to lead in the 21st Century Church that has created a pathway forward. That's the intellectual and mind-shift part of my journey. But the relational part has been even more important.

Chapter Eighteen

Communitas and Collaboration

Communitas

We have always known it is about relationships. No other organization on the planet is more firmly founded on the basis of relationship than the Church of Jesus Christ. In our 21st Century context, it is only the power of relationships that will see us through. It is such an ontological reality, our opportunity is to embrace these relationships. The power of the church is love in communal action.

What society requires of us is more intentionality and seriousness about our relationships. God's design is that the people of faith, followers of Jesus Christ, are to be the influencers of society. Alan Hirsch describes the groups that form as a result of this type of work not as being in community, but as communitas.[76] He did not create this word because it was needed, but reclaimed the word because it is reality. Communitas describes a group of people moving through some liminal space together. That is exactly what we are invited into.

152

Relatedly, Seel describes in *Network Power* two characteristics of group relationships that animate the forming of communitas. Paraphrasing his work;

Sociability

Within any group, there are varying degrees of obligation to one another, and some of these obligations become strong enough to grow into deep friendships. To the extent that this happens, this relational attachment to one another is defined as the sociability within a group. It is a measurable thing called network density, and has to do with the actual number of connections between members of a group, contrasted with how many connections could occur. In high density groups, group dynamics come into play and the group acts differently than any of the individual members. Commonly we can see community values versus individual values prevail, teamwork, and free exchange of information due to a higher level of trust. In high density networks relationships are King!

Solidarity

This is defined as each member's commitment to the mission or shared cause of a group. While we may be in a high sociability group, that does automatically mean that what we desire to influence in the world is the same, or if it is, that our commitment to doing so is equal. If relationship is King in Sociability, then mission is the Queen of Solidarity. It is the compelling purpose that keeps members of the group moving forward together, despite challenges.

This book opened with the story of the Cosby's *spoude'* leadership diligence to focus small groups to the mission group structure. The reason this structure cultivated missional change was the power of the communitas. In Church of the Saviour's 50 years, this structure birthed nine unique faith communities and a myriad of accompanying missions within greater Washington, DC. While the church is not at all famous, it is perhaps the most influential of any church, according to Jim Wallis of Sojourner's.[77] A sure sign of the power of a dense network is that it focuses on cause, not the leader. These mission groups are change agents as they combine high density sociability with high commitment to shared solidarity.

If our groups or networks do not keep the forces of sociability and solidarity in tension, they exhibit other traits. Mercenaries come from groups with high solidarity, but little sociability. There is little obligation to one another even though we can create some missional movement. This is dangerous as it provides the heroic façade of impact without the status quo being fundamentally challenged.

The flip side is high sociability but low solidarity. Here we are describing the typical church small group. The driving reason to be together is the relationship itself, to do community. The fallacy is that we will eventually turn missional. Here, groups connect within a church to form what looks like a united body. But without any shared missional focus between groups, and with others outside of the church, any power is dissipated. These are the types of groups the Cosby's discontinued supporting.

The fourth and final option are networks or groups low on sociability and solidarity. In this case its members are fragments that stay together as a bounded set because they know each other, or agree on some common ground, but have no power. It seems like there would be power when they gather together. But to look across a sea of people and hold the notion that well-intended accumulated individual actions will change the status quo is a fallacy. It just doesn't work that way. It wasn't designed to work that way.

As organization-building leaders, we can understand the components that make up these groups and networks, adapt our leadership to cultivate environments and facilitate healthy tension, share feedback throughout the network, reflect instead of react, connect through 'weak links' outside of ourselves and begin to see the movements we envision. Once we are committed to leading to this end, the visualization tools will be our best friend for sense-making and communicating these realities.

Collaboration

While relationships in communitas will be the hallmark of the people of the 21st Century Church, our institutional forms of organizations, in all sectors, will thrive through true collaboration.

A key area of collaboration for us is the unity of the witness of the Church. My friend Chris Handley,[78] a Transformative City Network leader, consistently asks how it is we can measure and visualize one portion of the Kingdom (our local church) while not losing sight of the rest. "Focusing on my church only reminds me of the ancient proverb of the elephant being assessed by two blind men, where each fails to account for the whole; therefore a wrong assessment."

Institutional collaboration is with and between the influential institutions of a given area. Each defined geography or people group has a few institutions whose influence is outsized, and any battle against the status quo that does not have them in picture is doomed. It's not that they are against change, but that they need to be part of the change. For we likely can all agree on the changes we desire. And that is the only space where collaboration is possible.

So what is collaboration? Here is what it is not. In Phil Knight's memoir on the creation of Nike, he required the company culture be what it took to win; for Nike. His worldview in business was formed running collegiate track at powerhouse Oregon. This perspective has served him, and many other companies, well. Phil noted the leaders that seemed most able to fit the culture were those that knew that art of war, that had a motivation to prove themselves and would never give up. For him, business was the next level of competition in life. War was the ultimate competition, but in his view, not worth the cost, therefore not to be pursued. Sport, business, war. And we idolize leaders in all these systems; which will not serve us well on the road to collaboration. However, it gives us an anchor as a place to contrast.

The contrast is well expressed in a continuum full of alliteration of how organizations choose to relate to one another.[79]

Competes	Co-exists	Communicates	Coordinates	Cooperates	Collaborates
Actively competes in similar activities for adherents, resources, partners, and attention.	Performs similar activities without input or exchange and will go on the offensive against others.	Leaders share basic information for mutual benefit and builds relationship via informal or formal connections.	Altering activities for a common purpose, as needed, often informally on discrete activities or projects.	Systemically adjusts and aligns work with others. Share resources (staff, finances, space, etc.).	Long-term interaction towards a shared mission, or goals. Includes shared leadership, decisions, and resources. Learns from each other to enhance each other's capacity.

Serves the Owners, Members   Serves the Common Good

From Competition to Collaboration Continuum

The fear many of us express when looking at the continuum is the loss of our identity as an organization, our uniqueness being stifled, and the possibility of being controlled by another. We are afraid of the complex power dynamics and not sure how to adopt a new mindset, especially when all we have known is competitive mindset. Yet we know this mindset produces the exact opposite of what we need to recognize: our interdependence. More than anything, we want our identity, uniqueness and contribution to positive change strengthened.

The churches and organizations that thrive in the 21st Century will be led in a manner that moves with intent and perseverance to the right of the continuum. We will begin to partner with anyone who shares the same goals and desires and is willing to take these steps. Additionally, we will be brutally honest with what we are actually doing. We won't say we are collaborating when our actions bely that. This is unfair to all involved, and ultimately will cause frustration leading to lack of confidence in our leadership.

Visualization of not only the relationships between people, but also between organizations is crucial; as each bind the relational fabric between people and groups of people more tightly.

Summary - visualization is important to help us see, make sense of and communicate two levels of relationship. The first is the communitas within groups of people, where sociability and solidarity combine to create change at grassroots level. The second is between institutions where collaboration will be the hallmark for fighting the power of the status quo at the strategic level. The network mapping processes and technology assist organization-building leaders function with and across both levels of networks.

Chapter Nineteen

Responsibility and Response

Our responsibility

Why do this work of redeeming measurement and embracing visualization? It seems like there is a lot to learn!

Let's remember the villain in our story: It is the power of the status quo–this system that has unthinkingly been built around two simple, easy to count measures. No individual clergy or local leader is at fault. No one of us can unilaterally change this. The easy problems have been solved, or as they crop up they are not the organization-builders role to solve. Seth Godin prompts us to consider that "difficult problems, on the other hand, stick around until someone with insight, dedication and commitment shows up and gets to work. Seeking our difficult problems is far more effective than avoiding them."

Jesus named it in the parable of the new and old wineskins. We are very familiar with the parable up through Luke 5:38, "No, new wine must be poured into new wineskins." He goes on to say in verse 39 "And no one, after drinking old wine, wants the new, for they say 'The old is better.'" He knew the power of the status quo and our likely response to it. But he moved forward, asking us to follow him and not be afraid.

When we accepted the role of local church leader, whether clergy or lay, we took on the mantle of care for a portion of the people of the world. For their lives we became partners with God in His work. These people are unconsciously trusting us to lead well, even when resisting our efforts. In our reflective times we feel the weight of that shared responsibility.

We are asserting a holistic path forward through this liminal space. A concern voiced is that this systemic change, while no doubt at the root, is very complex and time-consuming. What's wrong with just getting some easy wins? And one day, once it is simpler, we'll take it more seriously. Besides, we are not sure we can have any influence while we know there will be struggle. And truth be told, there is no complete answer in our lifetimes. Only future Church historians will be able to make any judgments about that.

Dichta of 60 Decibels frames a response this way: "The question is not whether taking measurement seriously is simple or complex. It is whether it is important enough to merit sustained time, effort and spirit to inquiry to persevere. The question isn't whether a more sophisticated and nuanced understanding is needed. The question is who will start on the journey first, thereby establishing an insurmountable lead on those who are happy to dawdle at the base on the mountain, in search of a way around or through."

Gordon Cosby never tired of inspiring and opening the imagination of the Church of the Saviour. Some 20 years after the mission group culture change, he encouraged the people of Church of the Saviour to live fully into their missions and calling, literally distributing the church in the city. It is a pro-phetic message to us today, summarized for length.[80]

Cosby asserts *that we need to deepen our trust level, for our problem is lack of faith. We ask why is there not more power* *from the gospel? Why is it we can't see it, experience it? Will it all come together? Is it workable? The answer is not the lack of the triune God himself, but that we are required to experience faith at new levels. Levels that allow us to be inwardly free to live in chaos and uncertainty and the pressure that comes. Not an abstracted spirituality but a deepening of faith that will allow us to bear the pressure gracefully and with joy. **There is no way out of the Call. It is not alterable– it is the nature of Call.** We are to be people of wisdom, whose judgment has matured. Compassion is not enough, but when we see what is happening, we must patiently build compassionate institutions and tutor apprentices. We need examples who are incarnating. It takes years to build wisdom, so we need to grow now. The problem is caution. We will go out once, but not again, and again, and again. Why don't we live into the promises of God? We will embrace risk-taking with abandon!*

So, if not us, then who?

Our response

While inwardly we have a responsibility to our call, the people of our times are yearning for a response from the Church. This is our unique opportunity, to claim in a new way the space the Church exists to play in our 21st Century world.

Referring back to the Church Cycle, Regele rightly anticipated the Faith Emphasis and Ministry Focus we are experiencing. He did not predict the unpredictable, however. He identified three areas that our responses as those with organization-building leadership roles today and in the coming years, will define. They are:

1. What will be the Church's status in society and what new forms and trends will emerge?
2. What structural examples will we see?

3. What will be the mood in the Church?[81]

This is very much in line with the five challenges for the Church that Loren Mead, the Founder of the Alban Institute, foresaw before his death in 2018:

1. To transfer the ownership of the church (priesthood of all believers)
2. To find new structures to carry out our faith
3. To discover a passionate spirituality (from knowledge of to experience of God)
4. To feed to the world's need for community (with loss of traditional modes of connection)
5. To become an 'apostolic people'

To the questions these bring up, discernment must guide our response. Discernment of the movement of Spirit, the desires of God, the life of Christ in any situation. Discernment is the role the Church can uniquely play in a community. It is the only organization set up to do so. Discernment is not democratic, consensual or hierarchical. It is a capability we need to recapture, embrace, and lead.

Data, measurement and, subsequently, visualization must reclaim their rightful place in this work. As we employ our human and financial resources in partnership with the Spirit, we are just discovering how to employ data. Amber Smart uses the DIKW pyramid to help frame the conversation between data and discernment.

The DIKW Pyramid

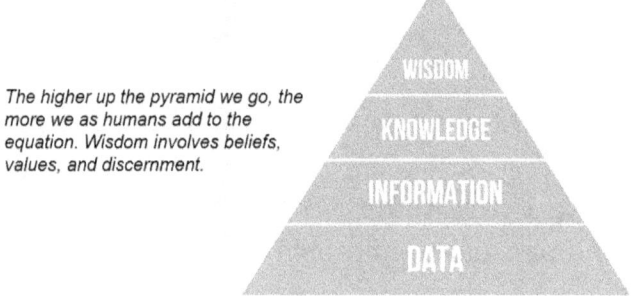

The higher up the pyramid we go, the more we as humans add to the equation. Wisdom involves beliefs, values, and discernment.

WISDOM

KNOWLEDGE

INFORMATION

DATA

"Data forms part of the foundation upon which we build awareness of the world around us." Says Smart. Ruth Haley Barton echoes this sentiment when she writes in *Pursuing God's Will Together* "the initial move of the listening phase of the discernment process is to *gather as much data as possible..* in order to *notice everything without judging.*"[82]

Data and measures are not the enemy of discernment, but a powerful perspective to enrich it. If we come to terms with the understanding that we don't know everything, that we have something to learn, then there is an opening to allow this new perspective. It represents the voice of the people, the hundreds or thousands or millions who have and will, through day to day behaviors, reveal insights and spark better questions.

Pastor Andy Morgan[83] in the United Methodist Church has been pursuing a renewal effort within a local region. While he knows he could quietly retire without doing the hard work of organization-building leadership, the Spirit will not let him rest. "For if you remain silent at this time, relief and deliverance will come from another place, but you and your father's house will perish. And who knows but that you have come to royal position for such a time as this?" This Scripture is animating his response. He does not want God to work from another place, but from His people–the Church.

Summary: We can't help that we were born when we were born, that we are in some position of leadership in the local church or related organization. Nevertheless, here we are. We have a responsibility to the God who has created and called us, the responsibility we assumed when we said yes. If called, God will see us through; he asks we lead with the zeal and abandon of *spoude'* diligence. For it is not about us. As the Church we are to respond to the liminal space, to the journey into the unknown. It is exactly the pilgrimage the gospel invites to take, for the sake of others to the glory of God. We have a reasonable pathway to follow. Let's go.

Chapter Twenty

Open Innovation and Invitation

Open Innovation

As we recall, this is not a 'how-to' book. No four steps to reclaiming organization-building leadership. No how-to change our mindset to redeem measurement. No three visualization graphs to bring to our next meeting.

Are there ideas on how to do these things? You bet. But they might not be the best. They might be wrong. They have been before. We really like them and they've gotten some refinement in the crucible of implementation. Many friends and collaborators have ideas too! Many of us have ideas, and are equally invested in advancing them for the common good. There are so many good ideas and initiatives it is hard to get our hands around them all. As a matter of fact, recent requests have centered around trying to get all these ideas in the same metaphorical room. To learn from one another.

So we are asking 'how to' questions instead. How can we collaborate to discover, learn, innovate, and see what emerges? How do we devise a framework to which all are invited to experience, contribute and be in communitas with those pursuing the same outcome? How do we innovate to create the future as we optimize our present and selectively forget the past?

Bishop Hagiya gives a hint of the way forward.

"In my estimation, the mainline church has valued mastery but not originality and innovation. The latter area has been off our radar screen as a church. This is probably the reason for our huge decline, as we have attempted to maintain our churches, not grow them... So, in terms of spiritual leadership, we must foster a balanced goal of artistry and originality.... Mastery without originality becomes rote; originality without mastery is faulty if not entirely random"[84]

He sees the two as interdependent.

"They feed and enhance each other in ways that can never be predicted. Every spiritual leader must reach outside his or her own comfort zone and take on a more innovative and entrepreneurial mindset. No less than the very existence of the mainline Christian Church is at stake."[85]

While writing to the mainline church, substituting any and all expressions of the church does not take away from the statement's truth. While the presenting issues vary among the traditions, the heart of our challenge is the same. As Regele points out in *Death of the Church,* contrasting the mainline evangelical traditions in 1995: "Both traditions are moving rapidly into a defining moment, and we would do well to heed Erich Hoffers' warning: 'in times of change, learners inherit the earth, while the learned find themselves beautifully equipped to deal with a world which no longer exists.'"[86]

In adopting an innovative mindset, we must take the next step to foster and embrace curiosity. As Smart talks with church leaders, she has named curiosity as the differentiating factor for church leaders that take the journey with her team contrasted with those that do not. "Curiosity is the super-power when dealing with uncertainty."

To belabor the importance, yet accessibility, of this point, Brene Brown guides us: "Choosing to be curious is choosing to be vulnerable because it requires us to surrender to uncertainty. We have to ask questions, admit to not knowing, risk being told that we shouldn't be asking, and, sometimes, make discoveries that lead to discomfort."

The way forward must give us a fighting chance against the status quo. These 'how-to' questions bring us to the next step: Who will do this work? Who is called to help create the future and willing to collaborate with others who desire the same? Who feels the responsibility to honor God's call in their life and vocation? Who wants the Church to respond as God desires for all people?

The 'who-to' are those that will discover the 'how-to'.

Are you curious?

Open Invitation

Kathy Merry[87] is a critical partner in this work. She shared aspects of this book with local church leaders in January 2023. Thirty people attended a five-hour workshop representing two churches exploring a potential collaboration. Afterward, she reported a personal sense of sadness, as the invitation to be curious and explore new questions was rejected in favor of trying harder at what was known. Three people, though, were interested, wanted to learn more, and were excited about the possibilities of thinking differently. However, they had nowhere to go with their excitement. Within those five hours, the status quo normed them into compliance, labeling them as outsiders. Their smoldering wick snuffed out. They will likely stick with their crowd, their congregation, alone. With a persistent ache in their heart and soul about what could be, might be.

This invitation is for those like them, like us. The curious. The committed. People desirous of pursuing their passions and call right where we are but have nowhere safe to turn. We want to participate in the innovation, the work God is doing. We sense there must be others but we are too distributed geographically and potentially hard to find. We are a layperson in a church, a staff member in a church, a denominational structure or non-profit, an ordained clergy person in any situation, a people disaffiliated with the Church as we know it but desire its beauty and impact in the world. We have not given up on it yet. We lead networks today but find ourselves stuck in repeating the same behaviors, knowing more impact is available. We do not feel called to abandon our roles, affiliations, and loyalties but desire to contribute to creating the future. Not just for ourselves or our organization but for the common good. But we don't see how. We are such a small part of the puzzle. We need a place to fit in.

The Preface described what was envisioned 10 years ago, the three interconnected areas we would pursue as the *rickety-bridge* mission group.

> *Visualizing the Church in new ways using the combination of science, art, and technology*
>
> *Transforming the people and systems of the church in ancient approaches yet fresh ways*
>
> *Thinking about, researching, and discovering new frameworks for practical church approaches that bring together the people desirous of the change.*

For those who think they might be part of 'the who', this is an invitation to participate as a person and/or organization in part three from above. That is the next step. The hub of this collaborative open innovation change network is *www.ricketybridge.org*.

Our shared cause is the reforming of Church leadership in North America, with ricketybridge the metaphor setting the expectation of what it feels like to do so. It will require a strong network of wise change stewards. We, together, will discover the work God is doing through us. The nascent framework will be available on September 1st, 2023. Each of us can contribute as called. All have a right to participate.

If you are curious, there will be five ways to engage based on your desire and capacity. Since these are ever-changing we will only provide a directional overview for this book.

Learn more about the concepts outlined in this book; re-imagining leadership, redeeming measurement and embracing visualization. All the resources that have informed this journey are here. This space will expand with our shared learning on these topics.

Contribute to the theology, practice, and add related disciplines and insights to further our understanding of why we must take this leadership pilgrimage, and how we might do so.

Connect with others who share your passions and desires, or discover those who care about the same cause but bring different gifts and skills. For those of us who feel alone in our desire and work of reformation we will find others in which to build our communitas.

Participate in building this open innovation network in two ways. One is to convene gatherings and invite others you know to share what what it is they learned and to refine and adapt our approaches to change together. Second is to opt-in to the experiment in the creation of the *ricketybridge* Atlas, a series of network maps. Chapter seventeen outlines the possibility. We will learn through doing.

Advocate for the *ricketybridge* open innovation network through the investment of time, talent and/or resources to refine and guard the vision, ensure its sustainability, model the leadership practices, convene the network leaders and keep the barriers to entry low. We will discover the patterns and emerging practices the Holy Spirit is powering on behalf of the entire network.

Participation on the ricketybridge change network will always be at no monetary cost, but it is not free. This work demands openness to new ideas and risk-taking. It will require becoming personally visible, findable, vulnerable and responsive. It requires learning the skills of reflection over reaction. It requires time from your daily, weekly and monthly rhythms. It requires adopting intentional practices that shift our thinking. It requires a willingness to be changed as we desire change. Like the reality of the gospel, it is hard, but it's worth it. We will continually invite one another into high-commitment structures for that is the only way change happens. We trust the Spirit will create through us what we can not do on our own.

Seel states in *Network Power* that "theory must give way to the local practitioner"[88] That is us, together, making the forms of Church for the 21st Century with and for all people practical.

For the curious, text 'bridge' to 804.488.9688 to share your interest and start the conversation. On September 1, 2023 we can also explore *www.ricketybridge.org.*

All are invited.

Act VII

Relationally, the foundation for the dream has been set through experiencing the network effects these forays have instigated. I list only a few examples to celebrate this serendipitous movement.

The first prototype of a network map was built for a person I met in the fundraising course in. Dwight Moody saw the network vision in Manuel Lima's *Visual Complexity: Mapping Patterns of Information* and asked me to mock it up and present it at his national conference. The prototype was built by Sean Gonzalez who I met in the programming Meetup and was funded by a member of the local church sending me to this work. A board member from that organization, Roy Craft, has become a mentor for this work for the past seven years.

The second network prototype was for a global denominational agency we met by serving in regional task forces. Relationships with engineers from graph database company Neo4J and network visualization software company Cambridge Intelligence met through the Meetups supported it at no cost. David Fauth and I went to Washington Nationals baseball games together, building our sociability and reinforcing the solidarity of our shared cause.

Initial *vizchurch* prototypes were created by a fellow employee at Starbucks, James Snyder, with mentoring from a two project managers and data scientist from the sending church. Data analysis and visualization projects for two non-denominational churches and a denominational project were facilitated by a data scientist, Steve Nock, who heard the vision while traveling together to a CrossFit competition.

This foundation building for the dream continues as it will never stop in our foray into the unknown and unknowable. The most important learning to date on all this is we can truly trust in the promises of God. We are at the current edge of the horizon of the story. The invitation to the *ricketybridge* change network.

You just met Kathy at the front end of the Invitation. As much as Jim Chandler helps get the cookies to where we can reach them, Kathy Merry is the partner with the strategic organizational perspective and creativity. We collaborate on all things. When either of us envisions a way forward, the other is invisibly there.

Since 2104 the three of us have wrestled with these questions. How can we help inspire courageous decisions for the good of others to the Glory of God? What can be learned through enabling new languages of measurement, movement, connections, relationships, and impact?

As an organizational participant of the *ricketybridge* change network, *encourageous* will participate in equipping church leaders in organization-building *spoude'* diligence and creating the tools to support this work. We see ourselves facilitating the movement of the inchworm described in chapter seven. The metaphor captures the pathway forward for all the people of the Church. Our work has taken us as far as we can go alone. We can only fulfill our call in collaboration with others. We need one another.

My vocation has certainly been non-traditional, from for-profit Fortune 500 management to local church leadership, small company presidency, local church leadership, to Church focused entrepreneurship and consulting, and now to exploring non-profit organization building. The call continues to unfold. But this part is unavoidable.

ricketybridge describes the reality of this journey and sets the expectation of what the journey will feel like for those who choose to participate. However, take heart in the words of the one who has built this rickety bridge, "Follow Me" and "Do not be afraid."

There is no retirement on the horizon. Why would there be when this is so much fun. Change in vocation, role, and function? Yea, for sure. But the work will go well beyond my physical life, and I will stay on this *ricketybridge* for as long as God wills; for such a time as this. Let's do this together.

Acknowledgements

This pilgrimage and book would not have been possible without two groups. One is my encourageous partners, Kathy Merry and Jim Chandler. Thank you for believing and entering into a dream that is still unfolding. The other is the rickety-bridge mission group, whose sustenance is a daily and weekly requirement. Thank you, Jim Melson, Jorge Forgues, Tom Pasmore, Chris Wimmer, Trenda Jacoks, and Michael Castrilli.

I could not be more grateful to the people of the two churches who embraced my mistakes and contributions to church leadership. Whatever lessons were learned were with them in the crucible of ministry, the highest of highs and lowest of lows. I appreciate that they never backed down from the hard work of leadership and accountability. There would be too many people to list; you know who you are. Thank you, Hempfield United Methodist Church and Crossroads United Methodist Church.

A special acknowledgment is to Jeff Kimmel, the churches he has been in leadership, and, most importantly, Centerpoint Church in Kalamazoo, MI. No one has been a more enthusiastic supporter of all the concepts of this book than Jeff, and it has allowed us to learn through experimenting. I am grateful to the leadership and staff of Centerpoint Church for allowing themselves to take the pilgrimage to 'learn a new way to think.'

The actual writing of the book happened in Writing in Community, a group led by Kristin Hatcher. This community with a shared goal (write a book) worldwide was a microcosm of the power of participation, self-organizing, and encouragement. I am particularly grateful to Jeff Gentry, Joyce Sullivan, Linda McLachlan, Titia Praamsma, Katharine Cartwright, Rachel Kelly, Trent Selbrede, and Win Treese for their persistent belief in me and assistance in the project.

Thank you to Matt Bates, Roy Craft, Edmund Lam, Tom Pasmore, and Eric Swanson, the initial readers of the book. You made it better through your inciteful feedback.

Other remarkable contributors to the content are Amber Smart, Andy Morgan, Anthony Deluise, Ben Roberts, Bill Edwards, Bob Strickland, Brian Barkocy, Brother Bryan Paquette, Cathy Norman, Charlotte Farmer, Chris Handley, Dave Norman, David Fauth, Dwight Moody, Eric Marsh, Gary Kendall, Glenn Colucci, Greg Gergen, Jeff Brandt, Jeff Porte, John Seel, Karen Sulmonetti, Kevin Kelly, Matt Angello, Mike Stevens, Monica Reynolds, Matt Engel, the Map team at SumApp, Nate Merrell, Paul Nixon, Ray Crabbs, Roland Fernandez, Ron Vandermeer, Sean Gonzalez, Seth Godin, Steve Nock, Stephen Hughes, Stephen Puracelli, Stuart Burt, Tony Bond and Wes Freeman.

The person who made this much more readable is Lindsay Yonce, my editor, collaborator, and friend, who is equally talented and gracious. Any errors are a result of my subsequent meddling. Thank you for your years of encouragement.

Laura, Marcus, and Cate, whose lives are hopelessly intertwined in this story, provide unconditional love and life. My love and thanks to you transcend this book.

Endnotes

Preface

1. Cosby, Gordon and Mary. *Mission: Possible. The Inward-outward journey of Mary and Gordon Cosby. An Interview.* (Interviewed by Jim Wallis. Sojourners Magazine, November-December 1997) pp. 16-22

Introduction

2. McKinney, Phil. *3 Types of Innovation - Institutional - Social - Technological* (Killer Innovations podcast, January 26, 2021)

- Institutional Innovation applies to organizations, teams, companies, industries and governments. Tends to get overlooked.

- Social Innovation has a positive social impact; usually driven by passion.

- Technological innovation are new products such as phones and software, etc. or scientific know-how, manufacturing processes, etc.

Chapter One

3. McKnight, Scot. *A Church Called Tov* (Tyndale House Publishers, 2020) p. 209

4. McKnight, Scot. *A Church Called Tov p. 209*

5. McKnight, Scot. *A Church Called Tov p. 208*

Chapter Two

6. 'Distinctionary' is helpful to describe how a particular word is being used in a particular context. How it is distinct from other definitions of the word without judging their value. It is particularly helpful when a word has many related but substantively different meanings.

7. From the philosophy of Management/Leadership of Roy Craft, friend and mentor with broad expertise and experience in multiple sectors, including religious. He sees the intersection of leadership and management integrated, as in an orchestra conductor. A conductor requires the good stewardship of professional management of individual

177

performers and section leaders and the deft touch of composite artist who brings forth the best of the best.

8. This is a descriptive term of function rather than a title or office. Those who perform these functions have titles such as Senior, Executive, President, etc. depending on the sector. We want to focus on the work that needs be done and this description best fits the re-imagining we need to do as church leaders.

9. Attributed to Lao Tzu, a Central figure in 4th - 6th century Chinese culture who's life and origin are disputed. The wisdom, however has bridged the centuries' as it gives voice to deep truth, to created reality. The beginning of the quote is "The wicked leader is he whom the people despise. The good leader is he whom the people revere" before moving onto the great leader. Other versions of the end of the full quote include "A leader is best when people barely know he exists, when his work is done, his aim fulfilled, they will say: we did it ourselves." and "when the best leader's work is done the people say, we did it ourselves!"

Chapter Three

10. Regele, Mike. *Death of the Church* (Zondervan Publishing House, 1995) p. 93

11. Hagiya, Grant. *Spiritual Kaizen, How to Become a Better Church Leader* (Abingdon Press, 2013) p. 62

Chapter Four

12. Hagiya, Grant. *Spiritual Kaizen p.19*

13. Hagiya, Grant. *Spiritual Kaizen p. 65*

14. Hagiya, Grant. *Spiritual Kaizen p. 125*

15. Cummings, Lee. *The Priesthood is Changing* (AriseShine22 Conference, Building Praying Churches for Revival Keynote Presentation, Radiant Church) May 2022

Chapter Five

16. Ephesians 4:1-16 is the perfect design for world transformation as given to us by Jesus as his identity and expression of calling. The gifts create a unifying effect to 'equip the saints for work of the ministry, for building up the body of Christ'. They are our identity as we practice the activity gifts (from Romans) of leading with diligence. For a fuller understanding of the latent power of this design please read Chapter 10 of *The Shaping of Things to Come* by Alan Hirsch and Michael Frost. To practically explore how to activate this power, connect with 5Q at www.5Qcentral.com

17. Frost, Michael and Hirsch, Alan *The Shaping of Things to Come. Innovation and Mission for the 21st-Century Church* (Hendrickson Publishers, Inc.) 2003 p. 171

18. Collins, Jim. *Good to Great and the Social Sectors. A Monograph to Accompany Good to Great* (Jim Collins, 2005) p. 12

Chapter Six

19. Godin, Seth. *Seth Godin on the Beatles, Why He Has No Staff, How to Change Your News Inputs and Future of the Planet* (The Carey Nieuwhof Leadership Podcast, June 15, 2022)

20. Regele, Mike. *Death of the Church* p. 34

21. Regele, Mike. *Death of the Church* p. 44

22. Eric Swanson's and the authors paths have intersected three times since 1992. The first was as Eric convened Externally Focused Churches with Leadership Network for a year-long learning community. A highlight was learning about innovation from IDEO in yurts in Big Sur, CA. The second as Eric convened Engagement Accelerators with Leadership Network and our shared curiosity about the use of data in church leadership brought us together as partners. The third is as Eric pursues the Transformative City Network city convening and advocacy as a mentor to the author. Eric has been been a steadfast supporter and you will see his work referenced throughout Leading with Diligence.

23. Regele, Mike. *Death of the Church* p. 49

24. Tickle, Phyllis. *The Great Emergence. How Christianity Is Changing and Why* (Baker Books) 2008 p. 14

25. Tickle, Phyllis. *The Great Emergence. p. 16*

26. Tickle, Phyllis *The Great Emergence. p. 27*

Chapter Seven

27. Ferworn, Alexander and Stacey, Deborah. *Inchworm-Mobility - Stable, Reliable, Inexpensive* (The Natural Selection Research Group, University of Guelph, Ontario, Canada)

28. Catmull, Ed. (Leadercast video presentation at Southview Community Church) 2014

Chapter Eight

29. For resource list follow the invitation in Chapter 20.

30. Swanson, Eric and Williams, Sam. *To Transform a City. Whole Church, Whole Gospel, Whole City* (Zondervan) 2010 p. 140

31. For an example follow the invitation in Chapter 20.

32. Swanson, Eric and Williams, Sam. *To Transform a City. p. 141*

33. Swanson, Eric and Williams, Sam. *To Transform a City. p. 141*

34. Swanson, Eric and Williams, Sam. *To Transform a City. p. 142*

35. Swanson, Eric and Williams, Sam. *To Transform a City. p. 142*

36. Swanson, Eric and Williams, Sam. *To Transform a City. p. 143*

37. Swanson, Eric and Williams, Sam. *To Transform a City. p. 143*

Chapter Nine

38. Regele, Mike. *Death of the Church* pp. 224 - 227

39. Deatrick, Tim. Mortarstone Generosity Training for local churches. Centerpoint Church. 2022

40. Ashoka builds and cultivates a community of Fellows, Young Changemakers, Changemaker Institutions, and beyond who see that the world now requires everyone to be a changemaker – a person that sees themselves as capable of creating large-scale, positive change. Together, amidst the exponential growth of a new inequality in changemaking at a worldwide scale, we mobilize (and accelerate) a movement to build an "Everyone a Changemaker" world where all people have the right and ability to co-lead solutions that transform their societies for the better. From Ashoka US website.

41. Seel, David John. *The New Copernicans. Millennials and the Survival of the Church* (Thomas Nelson) 2018 p. xxvii

42. Barna Group. *The Connected Generation. How Christian Leaders Around the World Can Strengthen Faith & Well-Being Among 18-35-Year-Olds* (Ventura, CA:Barna) 2022

43. Barna Group. *The Connected Generation.*

44. Godin, Seth. *Seth Godin on the Beatles, Why He Has No Staff, How to Change Your News Inputs and Future of the Planet*

Chapter Ten

45. John 6:14, NIV

46. Coaston, Jane. *Body Shaming Dressed Up as a Fitness Goal is Still Body Shaming* (New York Times, Opinion) November 6, 2021

47. As quoted by Sirolli, Ernesto *Want to help Someone? Shut Up and Listen* (TEDxEQChCh Conference Presentation) September 2012

Chapter Eleven

48. Davenport, Tom and Harris, Jeanne G. *Competing on analytics: the new science of winning* (Harvard Business Review Press) 2017

49. Bezos, Jeff. *Jeff Bezos Explains Why His Best Decisions Were Based Off Intuition, Not Analysis* (Inc.com by Isobel Asher Hamilton, Business Insider) 2018

50. McShea, Chris, Oakley, Dan and Mazzei, Chris. *How CEOS Can Keep Their Analytics Programs from Being a Waste of Time.* (Harvard Business Review) 2016

Chapter Twelve

51. Methodist data from Annual Statistics published annually in Annual Conference Journals. Episcopal Church data from Parochial Report published annually by the General Convention of the Episcopal Church. The non-denominational data from the *Church Data Dashboard Research Project Whitepaper* sponsored by Centerpoint Church, supported by Leadership Network and compiled by encourageous, LLC. June 2020.

52. Jacobs, Mary. *By the Numbers: United Methodists debate the use of church 'dashboards'* (The United Methodist Reporter) as posted on Willimon's blog Peculiar Prophet July 6, 2011

53. Jacobs, Mary. *By the Numbers: United Methodists debate the use of church 'dashboards'*

54. Willimon, William H. *Bishop. The Art of Questioning Authority by an Authority in Question* (Abingdon Press) 2012 p.54

Chapter Fourteen

55. Groeschel, Craig. *How to Measure Success Online.* (Life.Church Open Network video message) April 19, 2020

56. Panel participants were Lee Cummings, Jon Tyson, Corey Russell and David Perkins discussing *Birthed in Revival (AriseShine22 Conference, Building Praying Churches for Revival Keynote Presentation, Radiant Church) May 2022*

57. Blumenthal, David and McGinnis, Michael. *Measuring Vital Signs. An IOM Report of Core Metrics for Health and Health Care Progress.* (National Academy of Sciences) April 2015

58. Thorpe, Larry and Gourevitch, Marc. *Data Dashboards for Advancing Health and Equity: Proving Their Promise?* (American Journal of Public Health Volume 112, Issue 6) June 2022

59. Dichter, Sasha. *Time is on Your Side* (Sasha Dichter's Blog) April 21, 2021

Chapter Fifteen

61. The market leaders in online design education because the world's leading experts create our content and because we're specialized in design. From Interaction Design Foundation website.

62. Nightengale, Florence. *Florence Nightingale: The passionate statistician* (Science News, Julie Rehmeyer) November 26, 2008

63. Nightengale, Florence. *Florence Nightingale: The passionate statistician*

64. Seel, David John. *Network Power. The science of Making a Difference (Whithorn Press) 2021* pp 133

65. Simplified to compare the difference between a data as a table and a data visualization. A digital Sankey is interactive, in color and can be dynamic or visualized over time; none of which a printed black and white illustration can replicate. To see a live example follow the invitation in Chapter 20.

Chapter Sixteen

66. Data visualization pioneer Edward Tufte asserts Napoleon's March is probably the best statistical graphic ever drawn. Portraying the losses suffered by Napoleon's army in the Russian campaign of 1812 beginning at the Polish-Russian border, the thick band shows the size of the army at each position. The path of Napoleon's retreat from Moscow in the bitterly cold winter is depicted by the dark lower band, which is tied to temperature and time scales.

67. Seel, David John. *Network Power* pp 166

68. Seel, David John. *Network Power* pps 12 & 121

69. Seel, David John. *Network Power* pp 159

Chapter Seventeen

70. Popova, Maria *16 Life-Learnings from 16 Years of The Marginalian* (The Marginalian Newsletter) 2022

71. Capra, Christine. *It's a New Language That is Emerging* (sumApp website knowledge base help.sum-app.net) 2018

72. Capra, Christine. *It's a New Language That is Emerging*

Act VI

73. Jeff Kimmel is Executive Director at Centerpoint Church in Kalamazoo. MI. He held similar positions at Christ Church and Galilee United Methodist Church in Northern Virginia, where we met. He has been a partner in learning for for over 13 years and a collaborator extraordinaire.

74. Mike Harder is President of Concentric, a global Jesus-centric disciple making alliance. Mike and I met almost 20 years ago when we served together in Lancaster, PA. He has been a mentor and provided great insights into the work in his role as Executive Pastor in Philadelphia areas churches.

75. Tom Pasmore is Senior Pastor of Asbury UMC in Maryland and also served numerous congregations in Delaware. He is very active Conference

Leadership and has supported this work a regional church level. He has been part of the ricketybridge mission group since hearing about it in an airport in Jacksonville, FL in 2016.

Chapter Eighteen

76. Hirsch, Alan *The Forgotten Ways Handbook + a practical guide for developing missional churches* (Brazos Press) 2009 pp. 169-200

77. Wallis, Jim. *Mission: Possible. The Inward-outward journey of Mary and Gordon Cosby.*

78. Chris Handley is the Executive Director of Helping Florence Flourish of Florence, SC. Chris and the Board were early adopters of a workshop to get to the heart of measurement for their mission.

79. Contributions from: Mashek, D. *Capacities and Institutional Support Needed along the Collaboration Continuum* (presentation to the Academic Deans Committee of The Claremont Colleges, Claremont, CA) June 2015

Himmelman, Arthur T. *Collaboration for a Change: Definitions, Decision making Models, Roles, and Collaboration Process Guide* (Himmelman Consulting, Minneapolis, MN) January 2002

Chapter Nineteen

80. Cosby, Gordon. *The Need for Faith-based Servant Leaders* (Sermon of Church of the Saviour, Washington, DC.) 9/23/1990. www.inward/outward.org/sermon archives/ Bold is authors emphasis.

81. Regele, Mike. *Death of the Church* pp. 43-45

82. Barton, Ruth Haley. *Pursuing God's Will Together* (Intervarsity Press) 2012 p. 208

83. Any Morgan is lead pastor of Faith Church of Bellefonte., PA and one the very earliest encouragers of the authors faith journey. He has particular insight as he is also the author's brother-in-law.

Chapter Twenty

84. Hagiya, Grant. *Spiritual Kaizen* p. 117

85. Hagiya, Grant. *Spiritual Kaizen* p. 122

86. Regele, Mike. *Death of the Church* p. 52

87. Kathy Merry is the other partner with with the strategic organizational perspective and creativity. She has her own story to tell and works well with local churches and larger denominational structures. She is a co-author of *Does Your Church Have Prayer.*